# THE ELEMENTS
# OF
# INDUSTRIAL
# RELATIONS

*Jack Barbash*

HD
6971
.B34
1984

THE UNIVERSITY OF WISCONSIN PRESS

243835

Published 1984

The University of Wisconsin Press
114 North Murray Street
Madison, Wisconsin 53715

The University of Wisconsin Press, Ltd.
1 Gower Street
London WC1E 6HA, England

Copyright © 1984
The Board of Regents of the University of Wisconsin System
All rights reserved

First printing

Printed in the United States of America

For LC CIP information see the colophon

ISBN 0-299-09610-6 cloth
ISBN 0-299-09614-9 paperback

*To Kitty with love*

# Contents

# Preface

This book is built around the proposition that industrial relations is not only ideology—it is surely that—but also function. To be sure, industrial relations is each side's strategy in dealing with the other. But beyond that industrial relations is also a mode of inter-action or tension which maintains the enterprise organization in sufficient equilibrium to produce goods and services at competitive costs and create useful jobs. This is industrial relations as function.

This way of looking at industrial relations grew on me gradually in the course of talking to union and management people who were so preoccupied—understandably—with winning for their side that they were, it seemed to me, missing the larger context of their sit-uation: in an industrial society ruled by scarcity of resources some-body has to perform the management function, and when that happens, somebody or some group will perform the union func-tion. Further, however management and the union, or their equiv-alents, argue over their respective shares, there is nonetheless an essential interdependence which both sides have to come to terms with.

It is precisely the failure of the socialist systems to concede the legitimacy of the union or management function that accounts for much of their inefficiency and turmoil. This is essentially the meaning of Poland's agony. In our own situation, the bitterness which historically has accompanied labor problems is due in some measure to the failure to concede the legitimacy of the efficiency-security dialectic.

Following through on this reasoning I found that I had to con-front an additional question: what is there about the nature and structure of modern industrial life that invariably generates this conflict and tension? The fact that conflict and tension were also true of the socialist industrialisms suggested to me that capitalism was far too simple an answer. The symbiosis between industrialism and conflict, and the resolution of that conflict, is what this book is about.

My first systematic effort at developing a sort of logic of industrial relations was a paper delivered to a faculty seminar of the Industrial Relations Research Institute at the University of Wisconsin in the early 1960s, which became an article in the *British Journal of Industrial Relations* (March 1964) and, in turn, the basis of an IRRI course. The course went through several versions, but by 1971 I thought I had the material sufficiently in hand to produce a mimeographed edition. Since then I have written papers and articles which further develop themes and variations. I have borrowed ideas liberally from my earlier output in putting together the present work.

This book is not a rigorous Theory (uppercase) of industrial relations. Rather, it is theory in lowercase, or a body of concepts, judgments, values, ideas organized around what I hope is a coherent intellectual structure.

I rely only in part on formal documentation. I am also permitting myself the indulgence that seniority and direct observation of labor events over a long period justifies some leeway for intellectual freewheeling. So, this is not science that I am purveying here but rather an exercise in synthesis "with a broad sweep [and] a conspectus of a wide area," to borrow the kind of words of a reviewer of a recent other piece of mine.

I am in debt to so many people that I cannot, alas, acknowledge them all here although footnotes in their proper places will discharge some part of my obligation. I owe a great intellectual debt to the University of Wisconsin for allowing me to work in a stimulating and congenial atmosphere. I also owe a great debt to the Wisconsin "school" in the study of labor, which, as I have comprehended it, meant that the labor problem had first to be understood in the participants' own terms before useful generalizing could move forward. I never knew John R. Commons, the founding father of the school, personally, but he pioneered a way of looking at the labor problem that has never left me. I did know Selig Perlman as a friend, and he imparted an intellectual ambience that I hope I have been able to do justice to. I am indebted to colleagues and students in industrial relations who, over the years, provided the occasions for this enterprise and encouraged me to sharpen, test, and articulate its hypotheses.

My greatest debt is to my wife, Kitty, without whose help, good sense, and companionship this work would have been impossible.

JACK BARBASH

Madison, Wisconsin

# THE ELEMENTS OF
# INDUSTRIAL RELATIONS

# *Abbreviations*

AFL       American Federation of Labor
AFL-CIO American Federation of Labor–Congress of Industrial
          Organizations
AMA       American Management Association
CIO       Congress of Industrial Organizations
FAA       Federal Aviation Administration
GM        General Motors Corporation
IRRA      Industrial Relations Research Association
IRRI      Industrial Relations Research Institute,
          University of Wisconsin
IWW       Industrial Workers of the World
NICB      National Industrial Conference Board
NLRB      National Labor Relations Board
OSHA      Occupational Safety and Health Administration
TUC       Trades Union Congress, Great Britain
UAW       United Automobile Workers
USBLS     Bureau of Labor Statistics, U.S. Department of Labor
USW       United Steelworkers of America

# CHAPTER ONE

# Introduction and Preview

INDUSTRIAL RELATIONS can be defined simply as the management of labor problems in an industrial society or, more operationally, as the theories, techniques, and institutions for the resolution of contending money and power claims in the employment relationship. By this definition union business agents, NLRB investigators, labor arbitrators, personnel directors, industrial engineers, and professors of labor relations are all engaged in the practice of industrial relations.

If this work has a thesis it is that labor problems are normal, not pathological, in an industrialized society. Labor problems arise naturally out of the continuous interaction of management efficiency, work security, and public policy. This is an undertaking to formulate something like a coherent industrial relations framework based on these interactions.

Doubts have been expressed that the diverse behaviors associated with industrial relations are really reducible to a consistent structure. For Neil Chamberlain "the boundaries" of industrial relations are "obscure, and the reasons for drawing them not easily rationalized. The field sprawls and the territory . . . takes in a polyglot lot of inhabitants with diffuse and often separate interests . . . all the way from people with very real and operational problems of a how-to-do-it nature . . . to people whose interests are global in scope and abstract in focus" (Chamberlain 1960, 101). "Industrial relations," to George Shultz, "is problem-based. It is not a discipline in itself but rather draws on many disciplines for theory and technique to understand and help solve the problems arising in the work place, the labor market and at the bargaining table" (Shultz 1968, 1).

Nevertheless, there are grounds for believing that a more generalized foundation for industrial relations may be worth working at. The first is that industrial relations is an active field of practice—if not theory—dealing with many of the critical problems of the times. There ought to be available a perspective on these problems which permits both practitioners and scholars to see their work as part of some larger whole. At this stage of its intellectual development, industrial relations' limited theoretical pretensions may even have some positive value; it can keep the level of generalization close enough to reality to enable scholars and practitioners to see some connection between them.

The main point in favor of a separate industrial relations field is that no other field adequately covers the territory. In an earlier period industrial relations would have been just about the same as institutional labor economics, founded by John R. Commons and the so-called Wisconsin school. But institutional economics has only a marginal existence now, and mainline economics has no time for ideas that don't model well. Fields like organizational behavior are insufficiently related to the larger economy and society and, in addition, have taken a strong homilectic turn.

This work represents only a first step in fashioning industrial relations into a coherent field—the stage of identifying the constituent elements and how, in a general way, the elements fit into the total process. Industrial relations is seen as operating in the context of modern industrialism, defined as consisting of (1) technology or the production hardware, skills, techniques, and science; (2) scale, meaning large concentrations of investment in human and inanimate capital resources; (3) cost discipline, meaning the techniques of economizing on the use of costly resources in order to achieve an acceptable return on investment; (4) a disciplined labor force, meaning men and women at work who by education, training, culture, and motivation are responsive to efficiency techniques; (5) organization, meaning structured associations of people and the attendant rules to administer the technology, scale, cost discipline, and labor force under conditions of (6) uncertainty, meaning the unpredictability of economic events; and (7) the state, meaning the "overhead" facilitative, regulatory, procurement, and planning services characteristically rendered by government.

The key processes of industrial relations are (1) management efficiency or cost discipline, (2) a work society and union protectivism reacting against cost discipline, (3) management's counter-

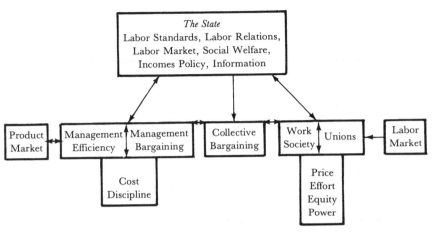

Figure 1. The horizontal arrows pointing in both directions between management and the work society/unions indicate that the parties are coparticipants as well as adversaries. The arrows running vertically in both directions in the management and work society/unions boxes represent internal bargaining *within* the structures of the respective parties.

protectivism in behalf of management rights or prerogatives, (4) the interaction of these processes through bargaining, and (5) state regulation and intervention. Figure 1 is an attempt to portray graphically how the key processes interrelate.

Management cost discipline consists of the deliberate planning, supervision, and control of enterprise decisions according to some standard of cost-profit or its eqivalent. Cost discipline in the labor sector comprises (*a*) professionalization and specializations in labor market administration, work performance, collective bargaining, and morale-building, and (*b*) controls which keep the labor sector in line with the economy of the enterprise.

Work society protectivism is the worker's necessary response to management cost discipline and the attendant tensions of (*a*) subordination, (*b*) competitiveness, (*c*) monotony and drudgery, (*d*) exploitation, and (*e*) economic instability. The acronym PEEP (price, equity, effort, and power) stands for the specific interests which the work society seeks to advance. The work society tries to get its way through one form or another of the withholding of effort.

Unionism is a special case of work society protectivism, but it is more formal and broader in scope and reach than the work society. The union's main objective is to enhance its bargaining effectiveness, and toward that end it engages in organizing, striking, negotiating, and governance. Workers' proneness to unionism varies, depending on (*a*) their bargaining power as individuals, (*b*) the threat which cost discipline presents to them, (*c*) the work group's ability to mount an effective response, (*d*) the employer's ability to counter that response, (*e*) the ways in which the external economy and society abet or discourage the forces of cost discipline and protectivism, and (*f*) workers' personal characteristics.

Bargaining is the strategy most commonly employed by management, work society and union to resolve their interests in conflict. Each side comes to the bargaining table because it needs something from the other side. Management needs efficient work from employees; work society and union want an acceptable PEEP level in return for efficiency. It is usually the prospect of losing what each side needs from the other that brings them to bargaining.

Bargaining is a love-hate, cooperation-conflict relationship. The parties have a common interest in maximizing the total revenue which finances their respective returns. But they take on adversarial postures in debating how the revenue shall be divided as between wages and profits. It is the adversarial posture which has historically set the tone of the relationship.

Nonunion groups are as capable of bargaining as are union groups. Although the work society may not bear the stamp of a union, it is nevertheless capable of engaging in the withholding of effort by regulation of output, absenteeism, tardiness, indiscipline, and—the most powerful sanction of all—leaving the job to take another. When employee groups organize as unions and engage in withholding, it is called a strike. The strike, latent or real, is now the foundation of collective bargaining.

The sides bargain not only with each other but internally as well. Neither management, the work society, nor the union is a monolith. Competing internal interests have to be bargained out before each side is prepared to present a unified front to the other.

In formal union-management collective bargaining the efficiency-security tension is partially resolved by a union-management agreement for a fixed term of usually two or three years. The quid pro quo's are management's acceptance of the agreement and the union's undertaking not to strike during the life of the agreement. The agreement is a detailed enumeration of mostly employee and union rights and represents the work society's PEEP correlate, so to speak.

The typical agreement runs to many pages and spells out (1) wages, hours, and the wage-job structure which the management promises to adhere to in the forthcoming period; (2) the rules of the work relationship; (3) the rights of employees on the job, most importantly seniority and discharge for just cause; (4) the rights of the union, most importantly the union shop and the dues checkoff; (5) the rights of management, typically the right of management to discharge its managerial functions except as modified by the agreement; and (6) the administration and interpretation of the agreement, most commonly through grievance-arbitration machinery.

In private sector bargaining the demands of the union and the response of management are eventually disciplined by the state of the product market, which is, in turn, a function of the state of the economy. A union typically will not pursue its demands to the point of pricing its members' jobs out of the market if it can foresee the employment effects. Reciprocally, the management is not likely to resist union demands to the point where management inflicts more harm on itself than on the union. Like the unions, managements don't, can't or won't always face up fully to the market implications of their behavior.

The state participates in industrial relations either to reenforce the interests of one side or the other or, in modern times, to enforce a general interest. The areas of state intervention are, broadly, (1) the labor market, e.g., "full" employment, education and training, employment offices; (2) labor standards, e.g., minimum wage, prevailing wage, occupational health and safety; (3) labor relations, e.g., the regulation of collective bargaining relationships; (4) wage-price stabilization; (5) social welfare, e.g., social security; (6) equal opportunity and affirmative action; (7) public sector bargaining; and (8) information, e.g., consumer price index, employment and unemployment statistics.

Management has found that some large part of its efficiency interests are served, and even enhanced, by catering to the security interests of the work society both in its union and nonunion forms. Similarly, the work society understands that its ability to achieve security is ultimately dependent on management efficiency. There is thus a reciprocal awareness that security and efficiency are, in some degree, functions of each other. It is the pressure of security on efficiency which forces management to probe the outer limits of labor economizing. Management resists excessive security demands in the interest of protecting or advancing its market position.

The strategic element in comparing industrial relations is the extent to which collective bargaining by the bilateral parties, backed up by the strike, is a determining force in wages, hours, working conditions, and settlement of disputes. By varying degrees collective bargaining in North America and Western Europe is more important than state power in shaping the terms of employment. State power is significantly more important in the developing societies and in the Soviet-type systems. Collective bargaining's importance seems to be a product of social democratic capitalism and its concomitant attributes of mass education and popular suffrage, a market price system, industrial relations professionalization, political pluralism, and the welfare state.

The industrial relations of all industrial societies, regardless of political system or "mode of production," contains a large hard core of management cost discipline and worker protectivism.

This work is mainly a series of propositions, concepts, and generalizations about industrial relations put together in a way to present a coherent if not always systematic structure of ideas. No formal or rigorous proof is attempted, although authority for generalizations is frequently cited. I do not offer a grand "theory" of industrial relations which demonstrates quantitative interrelationships, although the first step in any sort of theory is the identification of the component parts which are to be theorized about. This is what I try to do here for industrial relations and this is what I mean by the *elements* of industrial relations.

# CHAPTER TWO

# Roots of the Labor Problem

THE LABOR PROBLEMS of industrial relations are rooted in the essential structure of industrialism: specifically, technology, scale, the efficiency principle, organization, a modern state, and a committed labor force. More particularly, it is the way in which these structural features are manifested in postindustrial society that gives industrial relations in the United States and in the West generally its special character. Changes presently in the making suggest the emergence of a new stage beyond postindustrial society whose features can only be dimly perceived at the moment. But that is another matter.

*Technology.* Technology consists of (1) the "hardware" of production—that is, the tools, implements, machines, and electronics; (2) human skills, professions, crafts, and the organization of work flows; and (3) a system pool, or stock of applied knowledge and science.

It is common, with Norbert Wiener, to conceptualize two industrial revolutions. The first Industrial Revolution "concerned the machine purely as an alternative to human muscle" (Wiener 1945, 136). The second industrial revolution deals with "automatic machinery of the judgment-replacing type" (ibid., 159), what we now think of as automation, robotics, and data processing.

For industrial relations the fundamental effect of technology has been the division of labor and its tendency to create almost caste differences between manual and intellectual workers. Virtually every major aspect of industrial relations interconnects somehow with technology: the lessening of physical effort in work, the cen-

9

tralizing tendencies in the industrial organization, and a skill and employment structure inclining toward white-collar and professional occupations.

*Scale.* Largeness of scale is the second important feature of industrialism. Scale derives from modern technology, which, up to a point, makes large firms more efficient, profitable, and powerful than small ones. Scale also causes concentrations of business power, employment, and capital investment, and favors large plants. Large-scale aggregations of people and things are the raw material out of which complex management organizations and involved labor problems are made. Although depersonalization and tension are the inevitable consequences of the bigness syndrome, these are deemed not too heavy a price to pay for the economies of scale. Tension is not necessarily bad, but institutional arrangements are required to moderate it. The reduction of scale promised by the newer technologies will not materially reverse the depersonalization process.

*Efficiency.* Efficiency—or as it will be called later, cost discipline (or cost effectiveness or rationality)—arises in the first instance from the need to economize on scarce resources. In this sense cost discipline antedates industrialism. Modern cost discipline evolved out of "the hand-to-mouth existence of the peasant, . . . the privileged traditionalism of the guild craftsman and of the adventurer's capitalism oriented to the exploitation of political opportunities and irrational speculation" (Weber [1920] 1958, 76). Cost discipline became a science—or, at the least, a discipline or technique—when rule-of-thumb and folk wisdom proved inadequate. Cost discipline, as we shall see later, is the deliberate planning, supervision, and control of enterprise decisions according to some input-output standard, usually profit or some variant thereon.

Cost discipline can be as important as pure technology in affecting productivity. Dennison (1962, 232) notes:

> Managerial and organizational advances have recently slashed the requirements of holding inventories. The design of factory buildings has been radically altered to

permit the easy flow of material and that of office buildings to provide more usable space. Improvements in work scheduling, in personnel management and labor relations, and in methods of appraising and reaching potential markets are in this category, as are the whole fields of business organization and the management structure of business enterprise and other producing organizations.

Cost discipline under modern conditions also includes, as Galbraith has instructed us, "the need to control consumer behavior" (Galbraith 1968, 211). Cost discipline, accordingly, attempts "to prevent, offset or otherwise neutralize the effect of adverse developments, to insure that what is ultimately foreseen eventuates in fact" (ibid., 28). Most recently cost discipline has had to assimilate environmental deterioration into its theory.

Cost discipline is not limited to private decisions. Tests of cost effectiveness are increasingly being applied to public sector and other nonprofit enterprise. Indeed, the public sector has been a fertile field for efficiency reformers: scientific management, linear programing, cost-benefit analysis, and operations research were all first developed in the public enterprise.

Cost discipline forces a mode of calculation that creates an inevitable schism between cost consciousness and wage consciousness and a feeling among the workers of exploitation and inequity.

*Organization.* "The agents of production are commonly classed as Land, Labour and Capital," wrote Alfred Marshall in 1890. "It seems best sometimes to reckon Organization apart as a distinct agent of production" (Marshall 1948, 139). In operational terms organization means "lines of authority, . . . the distribution of people among different departments, divisions or other units, and the assignment of tasks to individuals and organizational units" (Whyte 1969, 61). Industrialism's technology, scale, and cost discipline demand specialized skills and professions and their assimilation into a production and distribution system which, except for the smallest enterprise, can only be administered by an organization. "The productive unit, 'the means of production,'"

Drucker has said, "is the organization itself rather than a material tool. . . . the organization rather than the individual . . . is productive in an industrial system" (Drucker 1962, 6).

In its simplest form organization may be conceptualized as vertical and horizontal. Scale in industrial enterprise imposes a scheme of vertical or hierarchical authority because there are limits to how many people one person can supervise. The complexity of knowledge and skill imposes a scheme of horizontal specialization because there are limits on how much one person can know. In addition, specializations must be coordinated; such coordination requires the establishment of an infra- or second-order organization whose primary responsibility is not efficient production and distribution directly, but rather, efficient organization, which in turn facilitates efficient production and distribution.

Capitalism's distinctive organizations are the private and public corporation. The principle of limited liability is the private corporation's great legal attribute; its managerial attribute is the ability to integrate the vertical and horizontal specializations into one entity.

The concept of the "technostructure" was invented by Galbraith to describe the locus of power in the large enterprise. In other times the technostructure has been called "the new class" and the "managerial elite." The technostructure "is an apparatus for group decision—for pooling and testing the information provided by numerous individuals to reach decisions that are beyond the knowledge of any one" (Galbraith 1968, 89) and is probably more influential than the management, the board of directors, and the stockholders, who are really decision-ratifiers, not decision-originators—and even as ratifiers their influence is likely to be marginal except in crisis.

Managers become so single-mindedly absorbed in their roles that an overlay of gamesmanship, professionalism, workmanship, and vested interest sometimes eclipses pure efficiency as the object of the organization. Management can take on an aspect of ideology to give its role moral as well as operational justification. The management role thus becomes an end in itself rather than a means to greater efficiency. As the employee and union responses also become institutionalized, we observe a game of industrial relations played for its own sake. The organization is deemed of such importance in industrial society that holding it together in some sort of internal equilibrium rivals efficiency in importance when equilibrium and efficiency conflict, as they often do.

Within the present generation new spinoffs from cost discipline—variously called administrative science, industrial relations, organizational behavior, and organization development—have emerged to enhance the state of the organizational arts and/or sciences.

*The state.* The state's functions in the industrial society can be identified broadly under five headings. In the *facilitative function* (Grether 1966, 9) the state provides the "social overhead" capital, e.g., railways, ports, roads (Rostow 1960, 24 ff.). The facilitative function also includes the laws and standards related to money, credit, and finance; weights and measures; trademarks, patents, and copyrights; incorporation, liquidation, and bankruptcy; and the collection and dissemination of statistics. The *regulatory function* is concerned with redressing power imbalances and maladjustments in the "markets for goods and services and for capital and labor" (Holton 1969, 45 ff.).

The *government procurement function,* especially in the military category and most specifically in research and development, has brought about a business relationship which "is more like the administrative relationship between an industrial corporation and its subsidiary than the traditional relationship between buyer and seller" (Price 1968, 281). Mobilization is now a "permanent arrangement" requiring the "continuous managerial supervision of a large segment of private industry and the continuous subsidy by government of the higher education of scientists and others" (ibid., 283).

The *economic planning function* belongs largely to the post-Depression and Keynesian era but is now threatened with attrition in the Reagan era. To be sure, this is not central economic planning of the socialist variety, but it is, nonetheless, planning in the sense of continuous monitoring of the economy for "full employment, high growth, price stability and balance-of-payments equilibrium" (Heller 1967, 59). In the postwar period, Heller observes, state

*13*

planning has moved "from a more passive to a more active policy made possible by steady advances in fact-gathering, forecasting techniques and business practice" (ibid., 69).

After full employment the state intervenes for redistributive objectives, as in the poverty program and for protection of the environment, as in the anti-pollution programs. The *social welfare function* has been represented traditionally in social security, public assistance, and establishment of minimum wages.

To staff these functions the state has had to become a major employer in its own right. In recent years (but slowing in the 1980s) state and local government employment has risen faster than federal employment, reflecting the larger importance of education and welfare in the division of government functions.

In a generation the state has advanced from the periphery to the center of the economy. Industrial relations has been profoundly affected by the pervasiveness of the state presence. Collective bargaining functions according to rules established by law. The terms of employment have to conform to legal wage and other working condition standards. The industrial relations parties function within labor markets organized through institutions like public employment offices and training agencies and guided by public policies for income maintenance, full employment, and anti-inflation. The state as employer makes the right to strike an issue in conflict.

At one time or another the state is an ally of business or of the working class. The state also intervenes in the economy to serve an independent "public interest," however defined at any given time, in which posture it is likely to find itself aligned against both employer and unions. The state thus becomes a third force in the industrial relations relationship, injecting still another set of institutional adjustments.

*A committed labor force.* Industrialism requires labor force "commitment"—that is to say, a permanent working class which depends for its livelihood mainly on wage employment. The attitudes and habits of the working class must be adaptable to industrial routines. Industrialism's workers need a basic education in order to read and comprehend directions and to make calculations. They need to be habituated to punctuality, regular attendance, and acceptance of authority. Also necessary is good physiological and mental health, and nutrition sufficient to support an acceptable work effort. The workers have to be imbued with rising expectations and a belief in the efficacy of individual effort to achieve these expectations. Arthur Young, an acute observer of the first Industrial Revolution, summed up the situation aptly: "Labour is generally *in reality* the cheapest where it is *nominally* the dearest; the quality of the work, the skill and dexterity of performance . . . must on an average depend very much on the state of ease in which the workman lives. If he be well nourished and clothed and his constitution kept in a state of vigour and activity he will perform incomparably better than a man whose poverty allows but a scanty nourishment" (Young [1835] 1965, 142). As a work force matures, management surveillance of the workplace to maintain discipline can be replaced by the worker's pride in "mastery of skills, then from job skills to sense of occupation, vocation and profession and ultimately to work as a career" (Fried 1966, 87).

These attributes of a productive labor force are encouraged by investments in social overhead or human capital (i.e., health and education), undertaken mostly by the state although in the earlier stages of development by the employer also. Other attributes, like work discipline and a work ethic, are generated within the individual himself from life experience.

"At the bottom of the uncertainty problem in economics," Frank Knight wrote a half century ago, "is the forward-looking character of the economic process itself" (Knight [1921] 1957, 237). The enterprise is subject both to uncertainties external to it—recessions, changes in consumer tastes, war, and social upheaval—and to uncertainties from within, as in internally generated innovation, imprecise forecasts, and strikes.

Protection against the risks of uncertainty becomes the first object of management cost discipline, the work society, and the union, each in its own way. The large cost commitment for the long-term future required by modern technology compels management to make its "highly strategic cost factors subject to purely internal decision" (Galbraith 1968, 29) and not to the vagaries of competitive markets. The work society's strategy is to immunize itself against the risks of uncertainty as far as it can through income and job guarantees. There may even be a convergence of interest in job security if management decides, as in the Japanese case, that this is the price it must pay for employee loyalty. Guarantees failing, the next line of defense is equitable rationing of the job risks which uncertainty produces.

Technology, scale, organization, state power, and uncertainty are the sources of the tensions in the work force which we designate as competitiveness, monotony, subordination, exploitation, economic insecurity, and physical deprivation. These tensions are examined in the next chapter.

# CHAPTER THREE

# Cost Discipline and Organization

COST DISCIPLINE is the key process of modern industrialism and the rules of the enterprise game all take their cues from it. It can be defined as the body of theory, knowledge, and practice which deals with how to economize on scarce resources in a systematic way. The discipline in cost discipline consists of the systematic planning, direction, and control of enterprise decisions, with profit or an equivalent as the ultimate arbiter of management success or failure. Although cost discipline functions under conditions of uncertainty, it continually tries to narrow the zone of uncertainty.

Cost discipline is derived from Weber's seminal concept of rationality: "It is one of the fundamental characteristics of an individualistic capitalistic economy that it is rationalized on the basis of rigorous calculation directed with foresight and caution toward the economic success which is sought" (Weber [1920] 1958, 76). Weber could not have fully appreciated that he was describing the characteristics of noncapitalist systems as well.

The term *cost discipline* comes closer than *profit* to describing what actually takes place in the pursuit of managerial efficiency. Profit is actually an operative calculation for only a handful of managers at the apex of the enterprise. Cost discipline—which, to be sure, has profit as its intended result—more aptly describes the continuous frame of reference for those lower in the organization; that is, each employee is governed by a more or less externally imposed series of quotas, goals, and objectives which are simulated profit equivalents. Only the executives at the very top are actually strategically located to manipulate all of the variables associated with the totality of profit. So, when we say that the distinguishing feature of capitalism is profit, what we really mean, in most cases, is that capitalism is a process of cost discipline which, if everything goes according to script, will end with some sort of profit. While cost discipline is apparently a necessary condition for profit-making, it is not the sufficient condition. Between cost discipline and profit there are imponderable intuitions and insights which remain in the realm of entrepreneurial art.

The sensitivity to costs represented by cost discipline did not, of course, begin with capitalism. But it was modern industrial capitalism that forced the transformation from sensitivity and intuitive awareness to discipline and, by some lights, science.

Cost discipline is a product of private capitalism which public and socialist enterprises eventually had to recognize as well. If there is a convergence between private and public sector economics and between socialism and capitalism, it is on this common ground. Cost discipline is thus approaching ''scientific'' status in the Marxist sense in that it has ceased to be an expression solely of the capitalist ''mode of production'' or ''class structure'' and has become the universal management standard.

Cost discipline in practice seems to involve five subprocesses:

1. Information: its accumulation, quantification and analysis, aptly identified in a recent work as ''vigilant information processing'' (Janis and Mann 1977, 4). Cost accounting is, in this respect, the first science of enterprise cost discipline.
2. Planning: in the classic words of Henri Fayol, written in the early 1900s, ''if foresight is not the whole of management at least it is an essential part of it. . . . It is a kind of future picture wherein proximate events are outlined with some distinctness'' (Fayol [1908] 1970, 123-24). The contemporary expression is ''corporate strategy,'' which for General Electric is ''How do you allocate resources for optimum growth?'' (Parisi 1978, 1).
3. Specialization of enterprise functions: accounting, marketing, finance, research and development, production, etc.
4. Professionalization: establishing the specializations as identifiable and certified bodies of theory, science, knowledge and know-how and educating or training a corps of practitioners in the diffusion of principles. ''Management techniques have be-

come more and more dissociated from the content of the activities in which they are used. These methods have been intellectualized to such an extent that they can be employed in the abstract'' (Crozier 1969, 150).

5. Control through organization and numbers: coordination of enterprise specializations so as to secure adherence to common cost, profit, or growth strategy.

As enterprise increases in scale, technological complexity, and geographical reach, the application of cost discipline exceeds the capabilites of the individual entrepreneur, and the horizontal and vertical divisions of labor set in—or, to put it another way, the organization emerges.

The wellsprings of enterprise organization are to be found first in the shift of production from cottage to factory. This shift induced a division of labor based on levels of supervision and authority. It also made possible a transforming technology which divided labor on the basis of knowledge and technique.

The ascendancy of organization meant the passing of the "captains of industry." Compare Henry Ford's observation that "there is no bent of mind more dangerous than . . . the 'genius for organization' " (Ford [1922] 1965, 141) to Alfred Sloan's "Much of my life in General Motors was devoted to the development, organization and reorganization of the governing groups in central management . . . required because of the paramount importance, in an organization like General Motors, of providing the right framework for decisions" (Sloan 1965, 435); or compare Ford to his grandson: "I'd like for my epitaph . . . an organization arrangement that will be stable enough and good enough. . . . That's the big thing General Motors has" (Serrin 1969, 156). The need for organization spurred the emergence of organizational consciousness and, ultimately, organization "science" based on the precept that "modern production . . . is not based on raw materials or gadgets but on principles of organization" (Drucker 1964, 31).

The application of cost discipline depends on the profit standard employed and then varies according to such considerations as (1) the phase of the business cycle, (2) the sophistication of the information input, (3) the cost and accounting assumptions, (4) the level of profit aspiration, (5) the complexity of the organization, (6) the organizational level at which it is being applied, (7) the time horizon, (8) the cultural setting, and (9) the degree of uncertainty.

The profit target can be formulated in absolute amounts as a return on net worth or in terms of growth, or it may be "not 'profit' but 'loss'—not the expectation of ending up with a surplus . . . but the inevitable and real risk of ending up with an impoverishing deficit, and the need, the absolute need to avoid this loss by providing against the risks" (Drucker 1962, 52). Profit or the avoidance of loss as targets may be interwoven with growth of assets or of share of the market.

Cost discipline tends to relax at the high point of the cycle and harden as decline sets in. The data which measure profits or other targets of maximization are not "objectively given" (Katona 1963, 194). It is simple enough to measure price or sales, but how measure the cost of a commodity? "Costs," Katona writes, "depend on depreciation rates, on valuation of inventories, on allocation of overhead, advertising, sales and developmental expenses. . . . How to apply the accounting principles, when to deviate from them, whether to transfer some 'profits' to special reserve funds or to draw on such funds—all this depends on subjective considerations, on the businessman's frame of reference and expectations" (195). The cost concept in the making is social cost whereby the enterprise is compelled, in effect, to measure the costs which it has inflicted on the environment and to incorporate them into its cost structure.

The level of aspiration influences cost discipline by setting a low or high profit expectation. The continuum of expectation ranges over Drucker's "loss avoidance" (Drucker 1962, 52) to Simon's "satisficing," to economic theory's "maximizing" (Simon 1969, 262) to the speculator's quick "killing."

The complexity of organization makes for complexity in the cost discipline process. The small proprietorship "operated as a source of livelihood for one or a small number of households" will aspire only to a living, a maximum of security, and a minimum of risk

(Chamberlain 1962, 49). As the firm grows in size, it is likely to (1) project its prospects over a longer period; (2) utilize more "scientific" planning and forecasting; (3) establish "subsidiary" cost discipline goals for the lower levels in the organization, stated variously as shipments, costs and cost reduction, and inventory turnover, etc. (ibid., 72); (4) seek "concomitant" goals parallel with profits, e.g., product quality, employee welfare, social responsibility (ibid., 74); (5) influence or manipulate consumer behavior; and (6) generate "internal bargaining" (as Walton and McKersie have instructed us [1965, chs. 8–9] within the management stratum as the diverse elements—finance, marketing, industrial relations, public relations, production, research and development—contend for resources and power. All this imparts a "political" dimension to cost discipline.

Something more about this last point. Although the formal source of administrative authority in the organization is the top executive, the large firm is "a mass of competing functional power groups, each seeking to influence company decisions in terms of its own interests or, at least, in terms of its own distorted image of the company's interests" (Strauss 1972, 7). Management "maneuvering and power plays . . . go on in the nation's offices and factories every day" (Martin and Sims 1964, 224). The maintenance of some sort of organizational balance frequently becomes as important as profit and, indeed, otherwise competent executives are let go because they aren't "team players."

The enterprise's time perspective determines whether it is out to make a "killing"—that is, a quick return, as in real estate or stock trading—or whether, as in the industrial enterprise or in the public sector, the time horizon is to be projected over several years or even decades.

The large enterprise has to live with both short- and long-term pressures. As Shonfeld has pointed out, "Management is overwhelmingly concerned with the long-term destiny of a great corporation in society, while many of the shareholders whom it purports to serve are solely interested in the short-term impact made by the corporation in the stock market" (Shonfeld 1969, 200–201). The state of business culture introduces such imponderables as business ethics, "concomitant" goals, countervailing power exerted by government, consumers, workers and competitive markets.

Cost discipline contains within it a large element of "art" and "vision," and pure entrepreneurship: "Art in the context of management, is above all the ability to 'sense' a situation: that is to respond to its nature and demands in terms of the inner or intuitive senses, which are capable of handling intangibles, rather than by assessing it with the equipment of reason, analysis and logic, with which the science of management must work" (Hooper 1960, 68). Schumpeter has argued that "rationalized and specialized office work will eventually blot out personality, the calculable result, the 'vision.' The leading man no longer has the opportunity to fling himself into the fray. He is becoming just another office worker—and one who is not always difficult to replace" (Schumpeter 1947, 133).

By now rationality in government administration is also becoming a fully developed field, discipline, or science. According to the ideal prescription of public sector rationality, "government should make decisions as systematically as possible—arraying alternative policies, assembling information on the advantages and disadvantages of each, and estimating the costs and benefits of public action. . . . Two major messages come through: (1) It is better to have some idea of where you are going than to fly blind, and (2) it is better to be orderly than haphazard about decision making" (Rivlin 1971, 2).

To be sure, public sector rationality lacks the discipline of explicit markets to coerce cost discipline, although efforts have been made to simulate marketlike constraints. Scientific management, linear programming, cost-benefit analysis, and PPB (planning, programming and budgeting) all had their origins in the efforts of government to economize and to justify itself. At the high point of PPB, for example, it was said the Pentagon "coupled hard-headed cost calculations with numerical estimates of how each program will benefit society," thereby enabling it to give priority to "the programs with the fattest social profit" (*Business Week* 1966, 122).

The theory underlying public sector economizing has been incisively stated by one of its leading theorists:

Economic analysis is concerned with the allocation of resources. Its basic maxim is: Maximize the value of objective received minus the value of resources used. In business this reduces itself to maximizing profits—both income and outgo being measured in dollars. In defense and generally in the public sector we lack a common valuation for objectives and resources and therefore have to use one of two weaker maxims— maximize objectives for given resources, or minimize resources for given objectives. (Hitch 1967, 14)

Politics if not economics has acted to discipline the demand for public goods. Voters have demonstrated that the demand for public goods is not infinitely elastic. Through initiatives and referendums citizens are imposing limits on property taxes and regularly rejecting bond issues and deficit financing. Marketlike signals have also been communicated by "privatizing" public goods— that is, by contracting out their production to the private sector or by changing user fees. These sorts of marketlike signals fall something short of the more measured responses of conventional markets, but even so, the signals have been strong enough to indicate that some public goods—like education, for example—have at various times priced themselves out of their markets in the calculations of taxpayers.

The origins of modern labor cost discipline was the factory from which it was subsequently extended to other types of worksites.

The factory . . . unites various kinds of workers, by mutual relations of control and subjection, into a compact and well-disciplined body, brings them together into a special business establishment, provides them with an extensive and complex outfit of the machinery of production, and thereby immensely increases their productive powers. . . . Under the factory system groups of workers of varied skill and equipment are united and enabled to accomplish the most difficult tasks of production. The secret of the factory's strength

*23*

for production thus lies in the effective utilization of labor. (Bücher 1919, 112)

The discipline in the labor process consists of (1) fields of specializations which correspond to the phases in the employment relationship, ranging from manpower planning and recruitment to "outplacement," retirement, and postretirement; (2) cadres of technicians and professionals—in accounting, marketing, finance, psychology, engineering, law, sociology, economics, industrial relations, and personnel—to administer these specializations; and (3) an enterprise control function which "measure[s] and correct[s] . . . activities of subordinates to ensure that these activities are contributing to the achievement of planned goals" (Koontz and O'Donnell 1968, 505).

The science of cost discipline and the state of the art are diffused through an external industrial relations "community" composed of schools of business, management and personnel associations, management consultants, and learned and popular periodicals, all engaged in active discussion, research, writing, education, training, professionalization, and indoctrination.

The personnel, industrial relations, or human resources specialization now "is a management function in the sense that finance or marketing or sales . . . is expected to make [its] contribution to profits just as any other function in the corporation does" (NICB 1963, 7). It commonly consists of five main areas:

1. The *labor market area* covers both the internal and external labor markets. The internal labor market matches labor supply and demand in the enterprise through manpower planning, recruitment, selection, testing, training, and personnel administration. The external labor market is influenced through employer association activity, lobbying, and wage surveys.

2. The *work performance area* classifies, measures, standardizes, supervises, appraises, motivates, and constructs compensation structures. Relevant specializations are job analysis, motion and time study, incentives, job evaluations, performance appraisal, and wage and salary and employee benefit administration. More

recently, public policy has forced affirmative action and occupational health and safety specializations. Quality of worklife with its emphasis on employee involvement and participation represents the most advanced salient in the human resources specialization.

3. The *work control area* "highlight[s] costs which are out of line" (Chamberlain 1965, 300) and supervises cost reduction methods. In a broader sense, control continually monitors the labor process for compliance with cost and quality standards (Jerome 1970, 316-19). One highly placed practitioner of control science compared the employment of controls "to flying an airplane. . . . You watched the dials to see if the plane deviated off course and when it did you nudged it back with the controls" (*Business Week* 1977, 68).

4. The *collective bargaining area* carries out enterprise policy in the negotiation and administration of collective agreements and seeks to affect the relevant public policy.

5. The *work morale area* functions to promote employee attitudes favorable to the company and work efficiency through training, research, counseling, communications, public relations, recreation and plant welfare and, in some cases, attitudes favorable to free enterprise ideology.

From the standpoint of cost discipline labor is a commodity; that is, labor, because it is scarce, represents costs and should be used economically. But labor is a special sort of commodity: it has a human being attached to it. As a consequence, all the employer can be sure of buying with a wage or salary is the employee's presence at the worksite and a presumptive readiness to work. In order to convert the employee's presence and readiness into efficient physical and mental effort, the manager must take the additional measure of motivation.

Motivating employees involves the manipulation or "fine tuning" of five variables: (1) the wage or salary and supplements, which, for the present purpose, we call the price of labor; (2) the diverse options for actually doing the work; (3) the work environment; (4) work attitudes; (5) the external labor market.

In the approximately two-hundred-year history of industrial work, cost discipline as applied to the labor process may be said to have evolved from lower to higher stages. The difference between the stages is the measure of discretion, autonomy, and control accorded the worker in the doing of the work.

The lower cost discipline minimized worker discretion. The typical Industrial Revolution employer paid a subsistence wage, not only because it was cheaper but because the employer believed that the worker would work only out of the "tyranny of necessity" and then only long enough to earn subsistence. "Everyone but an idiot knows that the lower classes must be kept poor or they will never be industrious," an Industrial Revolution employer observed (Rogers 1978, 15). Corporal punishment, fines, and continuous surveillance brought a prison mode of discipline to the work situation which fitted in with the employer's stereotype of the worker's character (in Malthus' words) as "inert, sluggish and averse from labor" (Malthus [1798] 1956, 89).

The early employer, practicing cost discipline at the current state of the art, sought to improve working-class morality in order to bring about industrious work habits. The work ethic idea served this sort of purpose. The workers in the Lynn shoe factories of the 1840s, for example, "were told when, where, how and for how much they must work; when and where to eat and sleep. They were ordered to attend church for which they had to pay pew rent; they were discharged for immoral conduct, for bad language, for disrespect, for attending dancing lessons, or for any cause that the agents or overseers thought sufficient. When thus discharged they were blacklisted and could obtain no employment in any corporation in Lowell or nearby towns" (Ware [1924] 1964, 107). Henry Ford's "profit-sharing system," John R. Commons remarked in 1919, "is a distribution not to men who are efficient in order to increase the output, but to men who lead a 'clean and wholesome life'—they get the profit" (Commons 1921, 11).

Industrialism in full swing—in the United States, in the post–Civil War era—brought with it a gradual lessening of the oppressiveness of work. Subsequently, trade unionism, professionalized management, factory inspection, work-easing technologies, and pervasive labor scarcity began to improve the work environment. Work's onerousness also diminished as backbreaking jobs began to give way to crafts and professions.

*26*

Formal cost discipline in the labor process probably begins with Frederick Taylor, who announced, as the century was turning, that "under scientific management arbitrary power ceases. . . . Every single subject, large and small, becomes a question for scientific investigation, for reduction to law" (Taylor [1911] 1947, 212). In Taylor's law the managers "assume[d] the burden of gathering together all of the traditional knowledge which in the past had been possessed by the workmen and then . . . classifying, tabulating and reducing this knowledge to rules, laws and formulae" (Walker 1968, 58).

Elton Mayo was the seminal thinker who introduced the next stage in the theory of labor cost discipline. Mayo rejected Taylor's economism, faulting employers for their view of "workmen . . . as a mere item in the cost of production rather than as a citizen fulfilling a social function. No increases in wages or improvement of working conditions can atone for the loss of real autonomy and of all sense of social function" (Mayo [1919] 1970, 130).

Mayo and the Hawthorne investigation which he inspired transformed the theory and practice of American work management. Taylorism still remains the hard core of cost discipline in the labor process for all industrialisms, irrespective of capitalist or socialist "modes of production." Managers still classify, tabulate, and reduce work "to rules, laws and formulae."

What has changed—and human relations theory has been important in paving the way—is the awareness of the human essence of the labor commodity and a continuing effort to enlarge the worker's say in his work. This is probably more applicable to white-collar, technical, professional, and creative workers than to manual workers. Refinements on the human relations theme have been introduced by such seminal thinkers as Abraham Maslow (self-actualization), Frederick Herzberg (the importance of the work itself), Douglas McGregor (Theory Y), and John Goldthorpe et al. (work as a means to an end, not an end in itself).

*Work in America*, the Health, Education and Welfare Department task force report, stressed the job discontent that permeated the industrial labor force and undoubtedly set the stage for the American quality of worklife movement which burst forth in the 1970s. The investigations of Britain's Tavistock Institute have come closest to establishing human relations as an integrated doctrine with the institute's "socio-technical system" model and the idea that both components are subject to adjustment and direction. "The problem was neither . . . simply 'adjustment' of people to technology nor technology to people but organizing the interface so that the best match could be obtained between both" (Trist 1976, 85).

The intellectual current that runs throughout the history of human relations is alienation in work, a theme which Marx brought into being almost a century and a half ago. All of these works represent the foundations of the emerging field of organizational behavior. Organizational behavior is the "effort to improve organizational effectiveness through long-term, planned, systematic applications of behavioral science, knowledge and techniques with the collaborative aid of skilled consultants" (Miles 1974, 165).

Not all of these theories and ideas rest comfortably under the human relations rubric, mostly because classical human relations takes the technical system as given—which Tavistock, for example, does not. The terms "humanization of work" and "quality of worklife" carry somewhat different connotations but not in any practical way. They are all human relations in effect, if not in strict definition, in that they all have in common (1) the need to make cost discipline techniques more responsive to the human dimension of the labor commodity in view of the increasingly intellectual content of work, (2) the centrality of self-actualization, autonomy, and discretion in the human dimension of work, but withal (3) the necessary constraints put on all human relations by a bottom line of some sort. By and large, the cash nexus in work is hardly ever made explicit by human relations theoreticians, with possibly mischievous consequences, as in the now commonplace criticism of the trade union preoccupation with "more," as if human relations were somehow above "more" for management—which it isn't.

None of this is meant to put down human relations; human relations "consciousness" has, without question, contributed much to lessen the oppressiveness of work. Nor should Taylor be unduly put down either, as is the vogue. Taylor's insistence that "more," which can take many forms, is a ruling motivation in work, has injected a useful realism in the work discussion, which otherwise has a tendency to ignore "more" as perhaps unworthy of genuinely committed workers.

There have been commentators, notably in Western Europe, who almost seemed to be saying that in any really humane society, human needs have to take precedence over economic constraints— that is, the maintenance of a humane quality of worklife must transcend cost discipline considerations. But the severe recession-depression that swept over the Western economies in the early 1980s has muted this undercurrent for the time being. Humane work for its own sake, however one might have expected it, has never been a serious goal of the socialist systems because there has never been a time when they felt secure enough to afford it.

Modern cost discipline's theory of labor may be conceptualized as a new management ethic. The new management ethic here is on the same plane of meaning as the work ethic. But whereas the work ethic put the burden of responsibility for a fair day's work on the worker, the new management ethic puts it on management. Under this new ethic management has to *earn* the right to a fair day's work from its employees.

The reasons for this turnabout begin with the transformation of the postwar labor market from a buyer's market into a seller's market. Everywhere in the West labor became the scarce factor, and its consequence, wage inflation, became the first economic problem.

Several additional labor market facts led management to its new ethic. Rising expectations, full employment, and increased income security lowered the tolerance for menial work among the younger and better-educated participants in the labor force. The lowered tolerance took such forms as increased indiscipline, absenteeism, quits, and, in Western Europe, the importation of "guest workers" to do the dirty work which the native work force was rejecting.

At the same time organizational behaviorists and other social scientists were studying work, altering the ideological climate by putting down most work as "meaningless," "alienating," and "not fit for humans." Indeed, the work scientists purported to know what did make work meaningful and productive; namely, worker participation.

Operationally the new management ethic comes to this: Management must give employees more say in their work and work surroundings. It is in management's cost discipline interest to enhance participation; the implication is that this can be achieved without surrendering management rights.

The key word, therefore, in the new management ethic is *participation,* as in participative management. The personal involvement which comes with participation, the logic runs, makes for both improved efficiency and more satisfying work. Participation may be individual, as in management by objective, or it may be collective, as in union representation in the boardroom (e.g., Chrysler, Pan American). Participation in these contexts is meant to be positive, affirmative, and problem-solving, and distinguishable from the protective, defensive, zero-sum collective bargaining approach to participation.

Another principle of work humanization or quality of worklife that informs the new management ethic is the enlargement of employee choice, through, for example, job rotation, flexible work schedules, and autonomous work groups. The ethic's decentralization principle—as in autonomous work groups—is based on the premise that the most effective and job-satisfying decision is likely to be made by those who are as close to the problem as is feasible.

The design of work used to be, in the Tayloristic scheme of things, an engineering decision. But the more modern view teaches us that there is also a large element of power in work design. "The work itself" becomes oppressive not only because of fatiguing physical movements but because of repetitiveness, short time cycles, uniform pacing, and detailed specification of tasks: All have in common the "simplification" of human discretion out of the work.

The theory of "socio-technical systems," identified with Britain's Tavistock Institute, does not focus so much on the precise work motions as it does on the necessary accommodation between the technical work system and the worker's human essence. Socio-technical systems theory emphasizes the discretionary "rather than the prescribed part of work roles," and "the individual as complementary to the machine rather than an extension of it" (Trist 1981, 7). It is the powerlessness of individual workers to work out their own motion patterns that makes the work alienating, not necessarily the work pattern as such.

The new management ethic as a manifestation of the higher cost discipline is not only an "ideal type" but reflects a substantial body of practice and programs with characterizations like the following:

1. Job enrichment: "more autonomy and responsibility" (Davis and Taylor 1972, 245);
2. Job enlargement: "variety of duties" (ibid.);
3. Job design: "specification of the contents, methods and relationship of jobs in order to satisfy technological and organizational requirements as well as the social and personal requirements of the job-holder" (ibid., 299);
4. Job rotation: "changing work assignments without . . . redesign of jobs" in the interest of reducing monotony (Sheppard and Herrick 1973, 64);
5. Autonomous work groups: "small assembly lines or other natural work units . . . freed from the strictures of a normally hierarchically structured organization" (Whiting 1972, 6);
6. Management by objective: the participation of the individual manager in "setting his own individual goal . . . consistent with those of the organization as a whole" (Strauss 1972, 10);
7. Flexible scheduling: "employees choose their own hours," working a specified "core time" and accumulating a set number of hours each; otherwise they "come and go pretty much as they please" (AMA 1974, n.p.);
8. Organization development: "the effort to improve organizational effectiveness through long term, planned, systematic applications of behavioral science, knowledge and techniques with the collaborative aid of skilled consultants" (Miles 1974, 165);
9. Sensitivity training: "increasing awareness and responsiveness to immediate interpersonal relations" (ibid., 173);

10. Human resource accounting: "the process of identifying, measuring and communicating information about human resources within organizations" (Craft 1975, 23).

Cost discipline's luster has dimmed somewhat in this time of disenchantment. Serious doubts are being expressed in the business community and elsewhere as to whether what we have called here cost discipline is really all that rational and really the best of all possible business worlds. Some say that the decline in enterprise rationality is of a piece with "American pragmatism['s] . . . excessive reliance on technocrats, on statistical analysis and . . . neglect of goals in a somewhat compulsive preoccupation with ways and means" (Lewis 1981).

How could the Vietnam War, directed by David Halberstam's "best and brightest," come to such an ignominious end? The computerized models of the recession eighties "made the most colossal forecasting errors since 1945. . . . The economy, in fact, entered the worst crisis since World War II," according to Otto Eckstein (1976, 17). The environmental crisis has brought to the fore cost discipline's failure to count social deterioration among the costs. The disillusioned critics of social policy say that with all the effort and expenditures, bad housing, crime, drug addiction, and illiteracy still strongly resist rational social action.

Cost discipline, the critique runs, has been overtaken by its own pathology. The defense industries so relaxed or suspended the norms of cost discipline "that incompetence, extravagance or mismanagement are no threat to the [their] survival" (Silk 1972). A commentator in *Business Week* concluded that "an increasing number of giant corporations . . . have lost control of their costs, lost access to their capital, misjudged their markets, and diversified into lines of business they do not understand" (Cobbs 1975, 16). Cost discipline, in an uncomfortable number of instances, has had to be supplemented by such nonrational methods as, in the words of a *Fortune* analyst, "collusion, coalitions, monopolies, cartels, favoritism, discrimination, premiums, rebates, kickbacks, bribes and other side payments, playing politics" (McDonald 1970, 131); see also Jensen 1975 and Crittenden 1976).

Cost discipline may also have been overextended beyond its

competence. Talking about Robert McNamara's effort to rationalize the Pentagon and the Vietnam War, Halberstam observed: "McNamara moved virtually alone in an area where he was least equipped to deal with the problems, where his training was all wrong: the quantifier trying to quantify the unquantifiable. What had worked for him so effectively in the past, the challenge of his own civilians loyal only to him and their craft, to the existing facts and preconceptions, was missing. He had no independent information with which to compete with the military's information" (Halberstam 1973, 303-4). The cost disciplinarians—i.e., the managers—are charged by a current work with being "hopelessly short-term in their investment calculations, . . . uncompetitive in their pricing strategies, . . . economically obtuse in their cost accounting, . . . ignorant of foreign markets and . . . boorish in dealing with workers" (Meyerson 1982, 22).

E. F. Schumacher's observation about economics' limited range of vision is applicable to cost discipline: "Out of the large number of aspects which in real life have to be seen and judged together before a decision can be taken, economics [read "cost discipline"] supplies only one—whether a thing yields a money profit to those who undertake it or not" (Schumacher 1973, 40). Considering that the prime source of growth in the modern economy is not capital but knowledge and that organization is people, "no quantitative surveillance," Rensis Likert has said, "is maintained over a firm's human assets" (Likert 1967, 103). This may be capitalist self-criticism in the backwash of a recession-depression, or it may be something deeper.

Cost discipline, formerly thought of as a "capitalist tool," has also become indispensable to public-sector and socialist enterprise. Cost discipline still reigns, but it has yet to assimilate the imponderables of art and vision in its calculations. Applied to the labor input, it has had to take on heavy doses of social policy and ideology in which participation has become the key idea. There is no doubt that cost discipline has been a huge success in advancing efficiency, but it is becoming the victim of its successes as numbers become ends in themselves and its methods are stretched beyond their competence.

# CHAPTER FOUR

# The Work Society

Workers, meaning people who take orders at any level, react to cost discipline by constructing a countervailing "work society." The work society is composed of work groups in the shop or office or executive suite. Frequently the work group fuses into and co-exists with a union or, at times, goes against the union. The work society is distinguishable from the union by its informal structure and by its narrower base in the labor market.

Work as a basis of organization and association depends on the social acceptability of work, the consciousness of being a worker, and a physical environment conducive to human association.

It is only recently, as history goes, that work and labor have become socially approved. As Hannah Arendt has instructed us, the Greek and Roman roots of the word *work* are derived from the word meaning "sorrow." Work did not become socially respectable until the nineteenth century, with the emergence of the work ethic. The work ethic is now deeply imbedded in the industrial society and may be one of the most important reasons people work. More about the work ethic later.

A sense of working class consciousness as a bond within the work society emerged when workers, freed from the guild system, ceased to be independent producers owning the materials or means of production. "The whole modern organization of labor in its advanced form rests on a fundamental fact . . ., namely, the definite separation between the functions of the capitalist and the workman, or in other words, between the direction of industrial operations and their execution in detail" (Ingram [1894] 1965, 25–26). It was the factory which first forced workers into a cohesive work society: "The original organizer of the trade union movement is the shop, the factory, the mine and the industry. The agitator or the labor leader merely announces the already existing fact." (F. Tannenbaum 1951, 59).

The work society is largely a protective association to alleviate the tensions which enterprise cost discipline imposes on its participants. These tensions arise from (1) subordination, (2) competitiveness, (3) exploitation, (4) monotony and drudgery, and (5) economic uncertainty. The mainsprings of these tensions are to be found mainly in the technology, scale, cost discipline, and economic uncertainty earlier identified as the essential features of the industrial method.

The structure of modern enterprise, accentuated in the factory, necessarily stratifies the work force, and the subordination that results from stratification necessarily generates tensions. The relatively large labor force demanded by industrialism requires a vertical, or hierarchical, division of labor, since there is a limit to the span of control which any one supervisor can efficiently exercise if, as commonly assumed, the lower participants will malinger if not supervised. Although many employees in this hierarchy are both order-givers and order-takers, at the lowest levels most employees are order-takers only. It is in the nature of such organization to create great inequalities and become a source of unrest. Under the regime of hierarchy "management is constantly originating activity for" the workers "at the bottom of the industrial pyramid" with little opportunity for the workers "to originate back. . . . [The] people in the bottom positions develop some resentment against the people who are always originating for them" (Whyte, 1955, 234).

The source of the competitive tension is the horizontal division of labor which springs from the specializations required by technology and organization. More than that, industrialism by its nature proliferates specializations, which then become professionalized, and professional rivalry also becomes a source of tension. The diverse work groups who populate the specializations, Sayles (1958) observes, "compete among themselves for the available economic rewards" (155) and organize into "interest groups" (55) to increase their rewards. The classic division is between the production worker and the skilled craftsman and between the manual worker and the white-collar worker. Division within the work force also becomes linked with differences in color, ethnic origin, and gender, and this linkage sharpens already existing tensions.

The tension of exploitation—a feeling on the part of the worker that the monetary return for his labor is something less than he is worth or deserves—stems from the clash between employer cost consciousness and worker wage consciousness. To the employer the worker's wage is a cost; to the worker the wage is income and a standard of life which he tries to insulate from the uncertainties of cost discipline. The worker is at considerable disadvantage in bargaining the price and power terms of the employment relationship with the employer. The sources of his disadvantage are (1) his total dependence on wages, (2) the short-term employment contract, (3) his lack of savings and the perishability of labor as commodity, (4) the large number of sellers compared to the small number of buyers, (5) the inadequacy of labor market information, and (6) restrictions on mobility. (See Hare 1965, 34–48.)

That the bargainers are of different social rank further widens the gulf between them. The only time they see each other is as adversaries. By contrast, bargainers of nonlabor transactions are likely to see one another in family, neighborhood, religious, and political associations.

The tensions caused by feelings of physical "deprivation" in the work effort itself are "impairment, tedium and weariness" (Baldamus 1961, 124). Impairment "is the state of mind of a person aware of his physical discomfort caused by strenuous work" (ibid., 53). Tedium is experienced by manual workers and is caused by "the repetitiveness of light work," while boredom is experienced by the professional occupations (57–58). Weariness comes from the tedium of repetitive work, as differentiated from the coercion of prolonged routine work. "Office routines . . . are less coercive than factory routines" (68–69). The feeling of deprivation is generated by minute specialization which makes the worker literally, in Marx's well-known phrase, "an appendage of the machine." The price which "management pays for the work simplification, routinization and ease of supervision inherent in mass production work" is some measure of "apathy and boredom, as positive satisfactions are engineered out of jobs" (Strauss and Sayles 1960, 43).

The degree to which workers are, in fact, affected by boredom and monotony is a matter of speculation, given the scarcity of evi-

dence. A survey sponsored by the U.S. Department of Labor reported that only 5 percent of the sample singled out boredom and routinization in work as the "single biggest problem they faced on their jobs" (Herrick and Quinn 1971, 16). Blauner reported some years earlier that "there is remarkable consistency in the findings that the vast majority of workers in virtually all occupations and industries are highly or moderately satisfied rather than dissatisfied with their jobs." There are, however, differences in the degree of satisfaction (Blauner 1960, 353).

The tension of uncertainty derives from the general economic uncertainty that is a pervasive feature of all modern economies. Historically, uncertainty for the worker begins with his dependence, as Frank Tannenbaum observed, on money wages as the sole source of income: "As long as men had the greater part of their living in real income produced by themselves the uncertainties of the money wage could be tolerated" (F. Tannenbaum 1951, 147). The hourly rate, a product of cost discipline, which "a man's income can be paid to him an hour's worth at a time," further accentuates uncertainty (Chamberlain 1968, 262). Changes may be a way of life for management, but for the worker, "the appearance of something new, whether in the form of a new labor-saving device, a new incentive system, a new kind of supervision, or a new process, seems to sound an alert among men at work; they mount guard, as it were, suspicious in advance that the change bodes them no good. . . . Even when it promises them substantial benefit, they may still pull and haul and balk" (Selekman 1947, 111).

Alienation, which has become a generalized term for worker discontent, may be more of a literary than a work phenomenon. The burden of the evidence suggests several conclusions: (1) The concept of alienation probably exaggerates the feeling of deprivation which workers experience at work. Dissatisfaction may be more in point here. (2) Workers seem to be able to cope with dissatisfaction—which is what this chapter on the work society is mostly about. (3) Discontent seems to be characteristic of industrial work wherever it is performed. It is not unique to capitalism, as many of the alienation theoreticians have argued. (4) Although the alienation discussion stresses deficiencies in the *quality* of worklife, it is the *economics* of work that by most other evidence continues to dominate workers' interest. (See Levitan and Johnson 1973, 17.) (5) Satisfied workers are not necessarily more productive workers. The research demonstrates some association between feelings of work satisfaction and such objective indicators as turnover and absenteeism but not with productivity and strikes.

The tensions inherent in work necessarily impart a strong protective cast to the outlook of the work society. Worker protectivism is expressed in a short-run time perspective. More than a half-century ago Robert Hoxie observed that, from the worker's viewpoint, "there is no long run but immediate need" (Hoxie 1923, 262). "Working-class life," the Goldthorpe group noted, "puts a premium on the taking of pleasures now, discourages planning for some future good. . . . This emphasis on the present and the lack of concern for planning ahead are . . . encouraged by the view that there is in fact little to be done about the future, that it is not to any major extent under the individual's control" (Goldthorpe et al. 1969, 119).

Protectivism, in addition, encourages a kind of sectionalism or local-mindedness which narrows the worker's perspective according to where he happens to be located in the industrial hierarchy. "In industry . . . it is what occurs at the lower level, on the factory floor, that matters most to the worker," Blumberg (1969, 3) noted. " 'Job-control,' 'job consciousness,' 'shop rights' which to the workingmen at the bench are identical with 'liberty' itself" are classic phrases which Selig Perlman employed to describe the worker's field of view (Perlman [1928] 1949, 275–78).

Workers bring an underlying pessimism to how they view their work prospects. "The manual worker is convinced by experience that he is living in a world of limited opportunity" (ibid., 239). Working people pick up from experience a job-fund theory that the supply of work is finite and it needs to be prudently conserved and rationed. More work now can only mean less work later. In general, the higher up employees are in the occupational and organizational hierarchy the less they are likely to feel that way.

Worker protectivism generates interests which may be identified by the acronym PEEP—price, equity, effort, power. The price of labor comprehends not only the money which the worker gets in the pay envelope but the total structure of compensation, including paid holidays and vacations, health care and pensions, overtime, and so on.

The manual worker's primary interest is the price of labor. Work is perceived mainly as a means to an economic end. The Goldthorpe group concluded that "the tendency will increase for industrial workers, *particularly unskilled or semiskilled men,* to define their work in a largely instrumental manner; that is, as essentially a means to ends which are extrinsic to their work situations" (Goldthorpe et al. 1968, 174). The extrinsic end is economic advancement. The worker's connection with an employer is primarily a "calculative one; it will be maintained for so long as the economic return for effort is seen as the best available, but for no other reason" (ibid., 39). An American investigation concluded, similarly, that "work for many people has become more and more a means towards the end of earning a living" (Morse and Weiss 1970, 42).

The equity interest of the worker arises out of the tendency to compare oneself to others.

> Comparisions are important to the worker. They establish the dividing line between a square deal and a raw deal. He knows that he cannot earn what he would like to have, but he wants what is coming to him. In a highly competitive society it is an affront to his dignity and a threat to his prestige when he receives less than another worker with whom he can legitimately be compared. . . . The worker's attitude toward the rate of pay is more significant for many purposes, than the real income it provides. (Ross 1948, 51)

Equity, for Homans, is "distributive justice" (Homans 1961, 232). "Man in an exchange relationship with another will expect that the rewards of each man be proportional to his costs—the greater the rewards the greater the costs—and that net rewards, or profits of each man, be proportional to his investments—the greater the investments the greater the profits" (Opsahl and Dunnette 1970, 146).

*39*

Effort is the physical and mental exertion offered by the worker in return for a specified price. Workers "have made a bargain . . . in terms of reward for effort" (Goldthorpe et al. 1968, 84).

Power is having a voice in the terms of employment, or "the extent to which a person is on his own when he works" (Ross and Zander 1970, 67). If there is one thing about work the literature agrees on, it is that "far up on the list of factors making for satisfaction in work is the desire among all groups for autonomy, responsibility, control, and decision-making power on the job" (Blumberg 1969, 119). The psychological root of autonomy in work is the "egomotive— . . . the desire to achieve and maintain a sense of personal worth and importance" (Likert 1970, 321). For most workers the power which is sought is in the doing of the work; workers want influence at the level of the job more than at the level of the enterprise as a whole (Lawler 1970, 168). They do not put a high value on control at the apex of the enterprise. Or, in Selig Perlman's words: "To the workingman, the freedom that matters supremely is the freedom on the job, freedom from unjust discrimination, which enables him to face his boss 'man to man'. Compared with this tangible sort of freedom, the 'higher' freedom, the freedom to elect the managers of industry who are to supplant the present day private boss, or the freedom which the intellectual talks about, appears too remote to enter into actual calculation" (Perlman [1928] 1949, 290).

Power entails not only autonomy at work but the freedom to change jobs—something which is normally possible only under full employment and the seller's market for labor which full employment brings. Job autonomy thus has a significant macroeconomic dimension not fully appreciated by the work theoreticians.

The literature used to accord a high place to the sense of community in the work society's priorities. Community is the worker's interest in the personal associations of the workplace. The interest in the work community embodies Herzberg's "hygienic" or "maintenance" factors. The absence of hygienic factors "serve[d] to bring about job dissatisfaction [but] were rarely involved in events that led to positive job attitudes." Herzberg's hygienic job dissatisfiers were "company policy and administration, supervision, salary, interpersonal relations and working conditions" (Herzberg 1970, 89).

The Goldthorpe group assigned a subordinate place to the community values of the workplace. "The workers in our sample as a whole have a notably *low* degree of affective involvement with their workmates, and . . . they do not for the most part derive any highly valued 'social' satisfactions from the existing face-to-face relationships of their workplace" (Goldthorpe et al. 1968, 52). Given the primacy of the economic interest in work, this report continued, "it is not surprising that, in general, they show no great concern over maintaining stable relationships with any particular set of workmates" (53).

Over and above PEEP, work may be seen as a way of life which is epitomized in the idea of the work ethic. The work ethic means that work is necessary to living, even for those who can afford not to work—or who don't need to work as much.

To begin with, work is undoubtedly physiologically necessary and is literally a condition of living. While there is disagreement as to whether a particular job is necessarily central to life, experience strongly indicates that some permanent attachment to the institution of work is central for almost everybody. Family relations, status in the community, self-worth, and mental health all require some settled work connection.

Yet, within our time, a mood has taken hold that the work ethic is withering away. Commonly cited as evidence are the overriding preoccupation with economic security and the decline of pride in work. Strong apprehensions are voiced about the casual attitude of the young toward work and their unrealistic expectations about it. Viewed with alarm also is the welfare "underclass" or "culture of poverty" with its aversion to work. The constant reiteration of the meaninglessness of work by the "alienation" school may have perversely lent itself to the creation of an antiwork ethic.

The work ethic thrived at a time when workers had only two options: work or starve. Given these limited choices, the work ethic idea helped to make a virtue out of stark necessity. But newer circumstances have changed our attitudes in a fundamental way. The choices are no longer severely limited to work or starvation. An affluent society—or at least a society of affluent expectations—has now made possible intervening choices, including such nonwork options as education, retirement, and social benefits which are just or almost as worthy as work. Under this more benevolent environment the work ethic has understandably lost something of its compulsiveness.

When one tries to test out the premise of a declining work ethic against what we know about the continuum of labor market behavior from entry through intermediate stages to retirement, no one firm truth emerges. Education has delayed the age of labor force entry, and social security has hastened the age of retirement. The most dramatic trend is the sensational increase in women's participation, but offsetting that, to some degree, are the erratic participation patterns of the young worker.

"Voluntary" unemployment may have increased because of unemployment insurance and the increased participation of youth and women. Hours worked per week and per year have declined, although some part of the decline is a statistical effect. Absenteeism has not increased significantly in recent years, and it is, in any case, again mainly the problem of the young, minorities, and women.

One may infer that the disproportionate involvement of the young, women, and minorities in manifestations of anti-work ethic behavior—let's call it—is partly due to the low-grade work which is their usual lot. (We make no judgment as to whether these groups are qualified to do more challenging work.) Menial work which is everyone's lot is one thing; menial work when almost everybody else is perceived as being more meaningfully engaged is another. It is possible, therefore, that another element in the changed outlook on work is the perceived meaninglessness of work where so much store is put in the meaning of work.

Although productivity has declined, much of this decline is a consequence of reduced capital investment and the changed composition of the labor force alluded to earlier.

Wages and hours in collective bargaining have moved in the direction of broadening leisure options. The anecdotal evidence that "people are less willing to put in a 'hard day's work' than they used to be" (Dennison 1979, 13) is folk wisdom, not evidence.

The welfare system has probably diminished the incentive to work in some degree, but it is not clear whether it diminishes work incentive proportionately to the amount of the payment. The evidence indicates that the more tenuous the labor market relationship, the more likely welfare will "buy out" the work ethic. In any case, it isn't that the welfare poor lack a work ethic—for poor families have a high proportion of full-time workers—so much as that their experience when they do work is not normally crowned with the success which is supposed to conclude the work ethic story (see Goodwin 1972).

To sum up: the psychological need to work cannot be as compelling under near-full employment, the welfare state, automation, and collective bargaining as it is under a grim work-or-starve option. Similarly, the incorporation of entitlement, leisure, the quality of worklife, and self-actualization into the popular value system is bound to discredit hard work as a way of life. What has happened is that workers can now aspire to better education, improved retirement, and a higher quality of worklife without loss of esteem. In the process the idea of work for its own sake suffers; so does the work ethic. The work ethic flourishes most under conditions of adversity. Paradoxically the work ethic seems to diminish as life's circumstances improve.

Workers' sentiments about work vary according to (1) how they perceive what their most urgent needs are, i.e., where they fit on Maslow's "hierarchy of needs"; (2) the demographic composition of the work group; (3) the technology of the production process; (4) the quality of management style; and (5) the condition of the labor market.

A. H. Maslow's classic hierarchy of needs arranges "physiolog[y], safety, love, esteem and self-actualization" in "a hierarchy of prepotency. . . . The less prepotent needs are minimized, even forgotten or denied. But when a need is fairly well satisfied, the next prepotent ('higher') need emerges, to dominate in turn the conscious life and to serve as the center of organization of behavior, since gratified needs are not active motivators" (Maslow [1943] 1970, 40).

In terms of reference employed here, the price of labor is probably the first need. "It is quite true that man lives by bread alone—when there is no bread'' (ibid., 28). When there is bread, he is likely to enlarge his need perception to demand longer-term security in the supply of bread, and perhaps to demand better quality bread.

Equity and power are the next higher needs, probably in that order. Power, autonomy, or self-actualization in work become dominant when the worker becomes conscious of his "human" need for self-expression, and that usually comes after satisfaction of the "lower order" needs of subsistence and safety. This needs-hierarchy model suggests that workers will trade off increments of lower order economic needs when these are largely achieved for increments of equity and autonomy.

The hierarchy of needs is not rigid: "When a need has been satisfied for a long time, this need may be underevaluated. People who have never experienced chronic hunger are apt to underestimate its effect and look upon food as a rather unimportant thing" (ibid., 36).

The upper-middle-class professionals who do most of the writing in the field of work are themselves ill at ease with pure economic needs and, therefore, tend to undervalue the importance to workers of these basic needs and overvalue the "higher order" needs. Taylorism's perception of the worker as an economic man has been the foil for much of this anti-economistic literature—more than the merits of his position warrant. There is more to Taylor's view of the worker as an economic man than the organizational behaviorists have been willing to concede.

Actually, economic needs are never entirely abandoned because in industrial society *all* needs are, so to say, monetized. Equity or relative standing among workers, for example, is in large part manifested by relative earnings, which are valued in this context far beyond their value in consumption.

A second plane of variation in attitudes toward work is demography. In general, there is a strong positive association between favorable work attitudes and occupation, job autonomy, age, and gender.

The major point of division in the occupational structure of the working class is between the "blue-collar" manual worker and the "middle-class," "white-collar" clerical, sales, technical, and professional employees. The manual worker "earns his livelihood through selling his labor power—through engaging in a direct 'money for effort' bargain" (Goldthorpe et al. 1968, 10). The white-collar employee sees his salary as emoluments appropriate to a particular grade and function and to a certain length of service" (ibid., 40). In contrast to the manual worker's interest in work as a means to an end, the white-collar employee develops intrinsic interests in work and in the work organization. This is the "bureaucratic" orientation, contrasting with the manualist's instrumentalism. In this orientation the relationship to employment takes on a moral rather than a purely market quality; there is strong "ego-involvement" in the work, and the distinction between work and nonwork is blurred (ibid.).

The white-collar employee, especially in the technical and professional categories, is better able to move laterally—that is, within the same occupation but from employer to employer—whereas the manual worker movement is mostly vertical—that is, upward within one employer organization. The bargaining power of white-collar employees vis-à-vis any employer is likely, therefore, to be greater, given the freer lateral mobility. The professional exercises the greatest control over the work, since the scope of the job is most likely defined initially by an external professional guild or its equivalent.

The social distance between white-collar employees and employer or management is narrower than between the blue-collar worker and management. White-collar employees and management are spatially closer on the worksite, work with each other in smaller units, and more often find themselves in association outside of work. There is still bargaining over price and power, but it is not embittered by social barriers. White-collar employees are likely to feel closer to management, when they are not themselves management, than to blue-collar employees. This is where the real rub of class may occur in industrial societies—not, as Marx hypothesized, between the beneficiaries and victims of surplus value.

The third plane of variation in work attitude is technological: the nature of the production process or the technical nature of the work itself, it is argued, makes its mark on the character of the work group. The most systematic development of this theme is to be found in the research of Joan Woodward and her colleagues. The Woodward thesis is that technical complexity—defined "to mean the extent to which the production process is controllable and its results predictable"—significantly affects "the attitudes and behavior of management and supervisory staff and the tone of industrial relations" (Woodward 1966, 12). The scale of technical complexity ascends from small batch and unit production (as in television transmitters and turbines), to large batch and mass production (as in automobiles), with process and continuous flow production (as in liquid gases and solids) representing the most advanced production stage in manufacturing.

> In the firms at the extremes of the scale, relationships were on the whole better than in the middle ranges. Pressure on the people at all levels of the industrial hierarchy seemed to build up as the technology advanced, became the heaviest in assembly line production and then relaxed, so reducing the personal conflicts. Some factors—the relaxation of pressure, the smaller working groups, the increasing ratio of supervisors to operators and the reduced need for labor economy—were conducive to industrial peace in process production. Thus, although some firms handled their labor problems more skillfully than others, these problems were much more difficult for firms in the middle ranges than those in unit or process production. The production system seemed more important in determining the quality of human relations than did the numbers employed. (Ibid., 49)

Blauner came to a similar conclusion earlier but by a different route. The research findings of the Goldthorpe group, however, do not support the correlation between technical complexity and the attitudes of work groups.

The affluent society with its base in full employment was the necessary precondition for the 1970s' quality-of-worklife movement and for the elevation of self-determination and autonomy at work into a high—if not the highest—priority demand. The problem of work quantity, which depends on the state of the labor market, had to be resolved before work quality could evolve from a utopian vision into a practical question. And by this principle the great recessions of the 1980s have forced the QWL movement to recede in importance, for the moment at least, as mass unemployment once again takes on the highest priority.

Workers are more satisfied with a participative management style than with authoritarian management. Whether they are also more productive is not quite as clear, although some organizational behavior research generally concludes that they are.

The building block of the work society is the primary work group. It is composed of workers who work near each other or who work at a machine together. Work groups seek to moderate cost discipline pressures and keep overzealous fellow workers in line. In the process, the work groups develop counternorms of work behavior which they seek to enforce on their fellows. (See Whyte 1955, 218; Perlman [1928] 1949, 242; Kahn 1958, 46: A. Tannenbaum 1966, 221.)

Work groups are essentially bargaining organizations with specific objectives and with sanctions at hand to pursue and enforce these objectives. The work society antedates the union and exists with or without a union. Where the work group coexists with a union, "at worst [it] play[s] an autonomous role, showing slight respect for the union or its policies." At best it meets "needs that the union disdains to consider, needs too petty and troublesome to be dealt with as union matters" (Kuhn 1961, 131, 132). The bargaining relationship is with the employer and, inside the work society, between work groups.

Bargaining between the work group and an arm of management is not always explicit, as when the union and management face each other in negotiations. Rather, work group bargaining is "tacit" bargaining "in which adversaries watch and interpret each other's behavior, each aware that his own actions are being interpreted and anticipated, each acting with a view to the expectations that he creates " (Schelling 1963, 21).

The work society and its work groups are continuously engaged in the bargaining of price, effort, equity, and power. However, the core interest is effort value—the relationship between effort and wages, in Baldamus's formulation: "Wages are costs to the firm, and the deprivations inherent in effort mean 'costs' to the employee. . . . A relative lowering of effort value is an advantage to management and a disadvantage to the workers, for it implies, by definition, that effort intensity per unit of wages is increased" (Baldamus 1961, 105). Bargaining of effort value is necessarily continuous. Since "the formal wage contract is never precise in stipulating how much effort is expected for a given wage (and vice versa), [the] details of the arrangement are left to be worked out through the direct interaction between the partners of the contract" (ibid., 35).

Supervision is really a mode of shop-level bargaining. "If a worker slackens his effort at one moment, the foreman's job is to remind him, as it were, that he departs from his obligations, and, in certain circumstances, it is quite possible that there may be some haggling between the two as to what is a 'fair' degree of effort in relation to the wages paid" (ibid., 36).

The effort bargain can be perceived as a function of the condition of the external labor and product market. Workers will work harder if they fear unemployment. Workers are likely not to work as hard if other jobs are relatively easy to get, and they need not fear replacement quite as much.

The work society seeks to subject the condition of employment to stability, predictability, and control. It "set[s] and maintain[s] a level of output or earnings which corresponds to the value the members place upon their efforts within existing conditions of work and pay" (Kuhn 1961, 132). Because the work society takes a pessimistic view of things, as we have already observed, and its biases are likely to be scarcity-prone, it tries to conserve the supply of work and employment (Leiserson [1931] 1969, 165). The work group tries to maintain its "integrity, . . . prestige," and, most of all, jursidiction in relation to the other groups (Kuhn 1961, 134).

Withholding of effort is the sanction which work groups employ to enforce their interests. The power to withhold, in turn, depends on cohesiveness. One type of withholding rations effort and output, the classic form being "restriction of output"—for example, work quotas, overtime bans, and "banking" (or rawhiding), which Kuhn defines as "working at a fast pace at one time in order to take it easy at another" (Kuhn 1961, 141). Another withholding type is not so much explicit rationing as it is a slowdown to protest a rate or quota. "Convinced that the piece rate is too low, the workers stand together to hold down production to hurt management and thus force an increase in the price" (Whyte 1955, 26). Withholding by restriction, whether as protest or rationing, "is a widespread institution, deeply entrenched in the working habits of American laboring people (Mathewson [1931] 1969, 146). Output restriction in one form or other "is so common as to be taken for granted" (Gardner 1946, 150).

If it has to, the work group will use sanctions to keep members in line. Ostracism, oral disapproval, and even physical force or threat of force may be resorted to. The work group relationship thus involves "control and conformity" for the members (A. Tannenbaum 1966, 61).

In addition to group efforts, individual workers may withhold effort on their own to express discontent. Tardiness, absenteeism, quits, and acts of indiscipline on the job, like thievery and low work quality, can be viewed as bargaining sanctions against management.

The current tendency in the research literature is to deprecate the importance of informal work groups as part of the general movement of human relations revisionism (Etzioni 1964, 46). A study of the assembly line found that "the majority of men . . . do not work in groups which are recognizable as distinct teams" (Walker and Guest 1952, 77). Nonetheless, there are groups of workers for whom work is invested with an important affective or solidaristic involvement (Goldthorpe et al. 1968, 40). Miners and steelworkers are authentic examples of the solidaristic work orientation. The "colleagueship" of scientists and professors is also solidaristic.

The tensions which workers experience and the protective responses which they resort to to alleviate these tensions are everywhere the necessary effects of an industrial order and are prior to the introduction of unions. It is the labor problem which creates unions, not unions which create the labor problem.

# CHAPTER FIVE

# The Union

THE UNION is a special case of the work society. Like the work society, the union is primarily but not exclusively a protective organization. The union differs from the work society in several important respects. Its government is formalized and its jurisdiction commonly goes beyond a plant or enterprise. The union coexists with the work society—sometimes in collaboration, sometimes in competition. The main point we make about the union is that its primary objective is bargaining effectiveness. The union's organizing, negotiation, striking, politics and legislation, and governance functions are all harnessed in the service of this goal.

Unionism in the United States emerged in the early decades of the nineteenth century, when the separation between masters and workers became evident and workers organized to protect themselves from the uncertainties and instabilities of the free market. In the United States the first unions were what we would call today local unions, organized by skilled craftsmen for protection against the "competitive menace" of "green hands" (Commons 1923, 220). In the United Kingdom craftsmen formed unions when the state-regulated skill standards were breaking down.

Sometime during the second third of the nineteenth century the American trade unions took on a strong anticapitalist coloration, associating the attrition of their skill investment with the fast-growing capitalist industrialism. The self-employed skilled craftsmen who formed these unions had not yet reconciled themselves to permanent wage-earner status, and their anticapitalism represented more an effort to preserve their autonomy than a commitment to a formal ideology. This anticapitalism was articulated mostly by disaffected—today we would say alienated—upper-middle-class intellectual reformers who, even before Marx, sought to channel the workers' anticapitalist, anti-industrial first reactions into producers' cooperatives, currency reform, temperance, and independent labor parties. In the United States the Knights of Labor, by 1886, marked the full flowering and then the rapid decline of the middle-class reform temper in American labor politics.

The passing of the Knights of Labor coincided with the rise of the craft union interest as the American industrial revolution got fully underway in the post–Civil War period. The American Federation of Labor, formed in 1886 out of a predecessor organization, became the symbol of this new unionism. The unionists of the post–Knights of Labor era based their strategy on these assumptions: industrial capitalism was here to stay; there was no retreat from wage-earner status; collective bargaining through working-class trade unionism was the best way to improve workers' circumstances; and if unions were to survive, collective bargaining, not wholesale social reform, had to be the primary function. This was what their "pure and simple unionism" amounted to.

Although the 1890s to the 1920s was the period of craft union ascendancy, there was no scarcity of socialist and syndicalist challengers, both within and outside of the AFL. The challengers rejected the idea that permanent solutions to the labor problem could be found under capitalism. The craft unionists' rejoinder was that they were not looking for permanent solutions.

But neither pure and simple unionism nor radical unionism could gain a foothold in the dynamic growth sectors of mass production—though not from lack of trying. The craft unions were able to flourish in construction, printing, and railroads. Their survival value as against their competitors has commonly been attributed to the relative weakness of their employers; their limited objectives; the strength of craft ties and welfare benefit unionism, which bound the workers to their unions in bad times as well as good; and the businesslike management of the union organization. The inability of the radical industrial unions to break through the barriers of big industry was probably due to the lack of state protection of the right to organize, the ferocity of employer antiunionism, and the unions' anticapitalist rhetoric.

The era of craft union dominance was brought to a catastrophic close with the Great Depression and the ensuing welfare state of the Roosevelt New Deal. This ushered in the modern period of

CIO mass unionism, marked by the penetration of unionism into the major sectors of the economy including, eventually, the public sector. Even in industries where unions could not prevail, the increasingly professionalized management was nevertheless compelled to take them into account in framing their industrial relations policies. Mass unionism in the private sector was mostly industrial unionism, and although the craft union prospered and even became "industrialized" eventually, it was the industrial unions who became the pacesetters in this era.

Industrial unionism, encouraged by the recovering economy and favorable legislation, embarked on an organizing campaign which probably tripled union membership. The growth rate declined during World War II, but this proved to be a period of consolidation of gains and the development of collective bargaining institutions.

In the 1950s the question began to crop up whether unionism had not reached a point of relative stagnation and even decline. It was against this background that the AFL and CIO merged into a unified federation, just about twenty years after their severance.

The question of growth was partly resolved in the 1960s when public employee unionism erupted to inject a new dynamic in union development. Union membership has continued to grow, largely because of expansion into the public sector, but membership has not grown by anything like the growth in the labor force. The critical deficiency seems to be the unions' inability to penetrate the white collar "proletariat" relative to its place in the total labor force.

Mass unionism has meant not only workers in unions; it has also represented a qualitative break with the past, bringing in its wake a complex system of collective bargaining, union power in the political realm, the economic enfranchisement of ethnic groups in industry, and, yes, also racketeering and a capability to hurt the economy by disruptive strikes and inflationary wage settlements.

The 1980s may be witnessing a major reversal of field as economic and political circumstances force unions into retreat.

The primary union types are, colloquially, "industrial" and "craft," or more precisely, inclusive and exclusive. The inclusive, or industrial, union takes in everybody or almost everybody in a plant, industry, or group of industries. The craft, or exclusive, union limits itself to a specified, more or less skilled group.

Industrial unionism's characteristic environment is a factory worksite, capital-intensive employment, high or middle-range technology, complex industrial organization, and national and international product markets. Craft unionism's environment is the reverse. Its nonfactory worksite is marked by low-level technology, local markets, and rudimentary enterprise organization. The complexity of industrial unionism's environment springs fundamentally from the large-scale character of employment and capital investment, which, in turn, breeds specialization of functions. Industrial unionism, being a product of a more complex environment, produces a more complex bargaining relationship and a more active and structured shop-floor society.

Because craft and industrial unions operate in different environments, their economics are also different. In order to support their high-wage structure, craft unions depend on regulating the labor supply flowing into their industry. The closed shop, the hiring hall, apprenticeship, and kindred methods are the means of regulation. The industrial union mostly regulates the supply of *work,* through work rules, etc., leaving the employer to control job entry. Industrial unionism's field of action in collective bargaining is principally the internal labor market of the enterprise, in contrast to craft unionism's main field of action, the external labor market.

The industrial union is also a different sort of social organization. Most industrial unions have had to assimilate the recent ethnic waves into industry. Because its industries are closer to the "center" economy, industrial unionism is also more closely associated with wide-ranging political and legislative programs in ways that the craft unions are not.

Craft unionism runs a simple industrial government. For most locals the business agent is effectively the union. Much of the rule-making in the craft union environment is unilaterally determined within the union, and work rules are, therefore, more likely to be found in the union consititution, by-laws, and custom, not in the joint agreement. The industrial union power relationship with management, by contrast, is more balanced. Craft union political aims are more job-oriented, and the response to new ethnic groups and women clamoring for access to their high-paying jobs has been more resistant.

Industrial and craft unionism represent more than inclusive or exclusive union organization; they also represent qualitatively different organizational, technological, and economic environments. The public sector union ought probably to be included as a third type or, at least a type 2½, since it partakes of the attributes of both types, leaning, it would seem, more toward the craft type. What makes public sector unionism—and, indeed, public sector industrial relations—different is the political essence of its environment and, therefore, a politicization of union and management. Not that private sector unionism does not have an important political dimension, but in the final analysis, economic calculations will resolve the relationship between the parties. The political essence of public sector unionism and of public sector industrial relations is that management and unions have to function at once and with equal force both in the economic *and* political spheres or markets.

The union is at its core a bargaining organization, and hence, what it seeks most of all is bargaining effectiveness. Bargaining effectiveness, therefore, represents the highest priority of the union leadership. For more than a century commentators have analyzed or advocated the union's primary goal variously as socialism (or conversely, capitalism), job consciousness, business unionism, maximizing (or "satisficing"), monopoly or organizational survival. The union does, of course, pursue many of these goals at various times, but these goals give way when and if they clash with bargaining effectiveness.

Bargaining effectiveness means the ability to command support from the rank and file, including striking where necessary, and the ability to command respect from employers and, in consequence, achieve acceptable gains from bargaining (Commons 1919, 15). Bargaining effectiveness is to be understood in the context of collective bargaining of the North American variety, where the union, as the designated and exclusive representative of workers in specified units, and employers negotiate the terms of employment.

The union's ability to strike—i.e., to withhold labor—and, of course, the employer's ability to withhold demand for labor are what, in the final analysis, bring the parties to the bargaining table. The inability of public sector parties to work out an acceptable role and function for the strike or, alternatively, acceptable impasse procedures are possibly the basic maladjustments in public sector industrial relations.

To be effective in negotiations the union must also undertake collateral functions of organizing, politics, and governance.

Organizing is essential to bargaining effectiveness because the union's ability to gain its demands from an employer is determined first by whether his employees stand behind the union, and then by whether the union has been able to organize his competitor's employees and hold them equally to union standards.

In general, workers join unions for three reasons: to protect and advance their wage and power position at work, to have a say in their working conditions, and because joining a union is required as a condition of employment. Once workers join the union under a union shop they seem to approve the principle on the equitable ground that those who benefit from the union should have to pay for it.

When workers choose *not* to join unions, it is because the labor market gives them greater individual bargaining power than they think they can get from a union, because they are afraid of the employer, because the employer, in effect, provides the equivalent of a union, or because the union is weak and ineffectual or appears so (see Juris and Roomkin 1980, ch. 8).

White collar and professional employment in the private sector continues to evade unionization. The fact that white-collar employees are not in unions is almost certainly not inherent in their white-collar status, as one may conclude from the large white-collar contingent in public sector unions. In fact, unionization of the public sector "middle-class" employee—nurses, doctors, professional athletes, teachers, airline pilots—has been one of the prominent features of the post-sixties era. The union impulse of the mass private sector, white-collar employees has been bought out, one may say, by a combination of tight labor markets which gave the white-collar group considerable bargaining power on their own, the automatic extension of blue-collar union gains to white-collar workers, and management's union substitution policy.

Employment in the enterprise involves participation in the work society as a matter of course. The worker's entry into the union is not quite as matter-of-course. If the union is already established, the closed or union shop and shop-floor pressure make membership in the union almost as automatic as in the work society. In the mines and on board ship the union *is* the work society.

"Union proneness" is used here to conceptualize the propensity of work groups to join unions when they have effective options to join or not to join. Union proneness is a function of (1) the worker's individual bargaining power, (2) the threat to PEEP posed by cost discipline, (3) the threat from competitive work groups, (4) the work group's cohesiveness, (5) the union's organizing effectiveness, (6) the employer's will to resist, and (7) the external legal and social environment.

Joining and organizing a union is, in most instances, a defensive response to a threat from the employer or rival work group. Most workers value the union not as a social movement but for what it can do concretely to advance their protective interests. For a small minority who "believe" in unions, unionism is perceived as an end in itself, that is as an instrument of social justice, if not of socialism.

Manual workers are more union prone than white-collar employees because they feel the need of protection from management cost discipline more keenly. Manual workers have less individual bargaining power, are more subject to the risks of unemployment, and exert less control over their work. Manual skills, except for the crafts, are not as easily transferable to other employments—all of which makes the manual worker more fearful of losing his job.

Many employees have the bargaining power to negotiate their own price of labor, but tenure rights, fringe benefits, and the like can only be negotiated collectively. For example, professionals in entertainment and sports are perfectly capable of bargaining their salaries on their own but have to turn to unions to negotiate rights and collective benefits.

Workers may be pushed into unionism not by an overt act of injustice by management but to protect themselves from a rival group of workers. White-collar employees sometimes become union prone in order to prevent absorption into manual workers' unions or because their relative position has worsened. Skilled workers will sever (or threaten to sever) their unit from a more inclusive unit to protect their relative economic position. Ethnic separatism from white-dominated unions is a relatively recent source of union proneness.

Union proneness may spring from a sense of need, injustice, and exploitation that has been heightened by the demonstration effect of militant action by others. The black civil rights revolution undoubtedly served as the example for the Chicano farm workers on the West Coast. The increased consciousness of women in unions—the Coalition of Labor Union Women, for example—arises out of the same source.

Teachers' and nurses' stronger union proneness since the 1960s cannot be accounted for by any objective worsening of their positions. More likely, unionism in these groups springs from a surge of awareness of how their professions have been "proletarianized" by a bureaucratized system. A sense of outrage generated from within also spurred the air controllers on to militant unionism.

All other things being equal, the higher the rank within the manual or white-collar class the greater the proneness to join unions. Craft workers, not the unskilled, were everywhere the first to organize unions. Professional employees, even if not in unions, have a long history of organization for quasi-union and technical purposes. Walter Runciman's concept of "relative deprivation" is in point here; it explains why the least exploited are likely to form unions before the most exploited: "Success . . . can provide the external stimulus by which comparisons are heightened, whereas those who are forced to adjust themselves to lesser achievements will reduce their aspirations in accordance with their experience" (Runciman 1966, 29).

Contrary to expectations, the low-paid are not strongly union prone. The evidence suggests that it is not the lack of union organization that produces low wages, but it is low wages and everything that that means which cause low union proneness; that is, the low-wage condition discourages union organization. Low-wage industries are marked by low profits, low productivity, high relative labor costs, small business, a marginal existence, highly competitive markets, and concentrations in nonunion areas. All of these elements create an enterprise which simply lacks the ability to pay and, hence, makes a poor collective bargaining prospect. Similarly, low-wage workers are linked with low education, low skill, and other socially disabling characteristics. These characteristics make internal cohesiveness more difficult and cause a vulnerability to exploitation.

Union proneness requires a sufficiently strong bond of sentiment among workers to enable them to respond to problems collectively. Many groups of workers are capable of self-organization into unions even before the union organizer arrives, in which case all the organizer does is simply formalize the fact. Less cohesive groups require help from without, usually from an "outside" union, to transform their inchoate discontent into something like a movement.

Until the civil rights movement generated "a sense of kind" among them, black workers found it difficult to mount effective union efforts on their own power. They seemed to lack "the solidarity of other occupational communities with an ethnic and religious base" (Wilensky 1966, 37). The communal spirit fostered by the church in the case of the Irish, by the socialist movement in the case of urban Jews, by nativistic feeling in the case of the Scandinavians, and by pride of occupation in the case of the Welsh and Scottish miners provided the cementing bond which is frequently a precondition of unionization. By contrast with black workers, the "earlier European groups . . . were not burdened with the tradition of slavery, with legal and governmental exclusion and, above all, with the visibility of different skin color" (Clark 1969, 130).

Craftsmen have everywhere shown a high-organizing capability bred by training, self-confidence, and easy mobility. The craftsman's bonds extend beyond the job to a more broadly based labor market. Historically, craftsmen's mutual aid societies paved the way for the union.

Broadly speaking, the union wants a voice in setting the price of labor, but it finds that in pursuing the full implications of that objective it must also secure a voice in how the labor is to be utilized. It is this consequence of bargaining that clashes with the rights of management, as we shall see.

To begin with, the union is not simply bargaining an hourly or weekly rate. When the union bargains provisions relating to job security—that is, layoff, recall, transfer, promotion, job, and earnings guarantees—it is, in effect, bargaining something approaching a career price. Discharge, just cause, and seniority provisions, even though classed as noneconomic, really go far toward determining how much a job is going to be worth over time to an individual. And the provisions relating to vacations, holidays, overtime, pensions, and health benefits also influence labor's long-term price.

The quid pro quo for the price of labor is the effort which workers contract to put forth. A price is high or low to the worker depending on how hard he has to work for it. Therefore, production standards, hours of work, and the intensity of supervision are all considerations integral to the price bargain.

The point is that unless the union can protest or petition for a review of any of the price-related terms—seniority, discharge, production standards—it has relinquished by that much its price-bargaining ability. Or, conversely, if the employer has a right to change these critical price-related terms unilaterally, the bargain makes no sense from the union's or the worker's viewpoint.

In short, the union has to have the power that comes from the right to strike to get labor price agreement in the first place. And then it has to have continuing power to demand accountability from the management on how the labor is being utilized. Finally, the union has to have power in order to establish a rule of rights and entitlements in the workplace to replace the exclusive rule by management dispensation.

For all of these reasons price and power stand in a symbiotic relationship to each other. The labor transaction only *begins* with the negotiation of the hourly wage; it is consummated only at the point that the union is able to review or protest applications of the wage principle to specific cases.

In effect, what the union has to have to back up the negotiation of a wage is management accountability, which is commonly but not exclusively enforced through a grievance procedure. Bargaining effectiveness is, therefore, put to the test not only in the negotiation of the agreement but even more so on the shop or office floor.

Unions impose two limitations on themselves in the interest of bargaining effectiveness. First, they deliberately restrict their bargaining to the terms of *employment*. Generally, unions acknowledge that they lack competence to deal with other management functions. Moreover, if they spread themselves into the other functions they would dilute the force of their employment bargain. Second, unions restrict themselves to a "grieving," protective, adversary posture as more compatible with bargaining effectiveness than co-management, partnership (now codetermination), or any other variation which puts the union in a position of co-responsibility with management.

This self-denial has little to do with ideology. It has more to do with the union view that it is likely to be most effective in bargaining if it lets management initiate and enters the decision-making process only at the point of protesting or "grieving" against particular management decisions. In the union philosophy, co-responsibility with management, even if management agreed, would undermine the adversarial principle to which the union is committed as a condition of its independence from management.

By the same logic, American unions reject ownership and control of the means of production as undesirable so long as the union is able to bargain with those who do own and control. In the union view, its bargaining effectiveness may, in fact, be impaired by codetermination because management will end up by resisting union demands to which they would otherwise agree.

The union view is that it is likely to get more for its people through countervailing power than by integration into the management system, which is what it fears from codetermination. Ideologically, American unions lack the socialist commitment which is the mainspring of codetermination. But again, it is not so much that American unions are procapitalist as that codetermination and its variants, including socialism, do not make out a case that union bargaining effectiveness will be enhanced thereby. For the European union movements, socialism may or may not yield superior bargaining results, but in some yet ill-defined way, social-ism represents a higher stage of working class development.

Circumstances alter principles, however. In the realignment of power that has been taking place in the 1980s some unions have had to reverse their stands on codetermination or its variants. Faced with the imminent insolvency of a major employer, the UAW, for example, took a seat on the Chrysler board of directors, not so much in the interest of codetermination ideology as to gain a voice in plant closings and other retrenchment decisions before it became too late to make a difference. Moreover, it may be argued that professional unions in state and local government have been achieving the effects of codetermination without using the word. These unions in health and welfare services have negotiated "con-tract provisions related to personnel policies including job descrip-tions, position classifications, work schedules, examination and promotion procedures, recruitment policies and training pro-grams. Many decisions long regarded by public employers as part of management's prerogatives have become bargainable issues" (Spero and Capozzolla 1972, 188). And many of the prerogatives go beyond the narrow confines of wages and hours.

"More" does not really explain much about what unions seek in bargaining. It does not, for example, begin to explain the ele-ments which go into the mix of the compensation package. In any case, just "more" probably represents a lower bargaining priority for the unions than equity. "Equity" means the maintenance of an acceptable balance among the contending claims of the sec-tional groups within the union and in relation to the "significant others" on the outside with whom the sectional groups compare themselves. To recall: "Compari[sons] . . . establish the dividing line between a square deal and a raw deal" (Ross 1948, 51). Equity represents some internal parity of price and power which is a condition of union solidarity in moments of stress. The union leadership ignores this balance of forces at the peril of severance and secession, or, at the very least, of lowered rank-and-file morale.

Bargaining excludes revolution. First, bargaining involves com-ing to terms with the fundamental structure of the other side. Employers will not come to the bargaining table to negotiate their own dissolution. Second, the high priority attached to *immediate* gains by the union's rank and file forces the union to settle for what it can get *now*. The postponement of incremental gains for a longer run socialist advantage is likely to cause disaffection among the rank and file, who live and think day-to-day. It was the recognition of this rank-and-file opportunism that prompted Lenin and other revolutionary theoreticians to conclude correctly that revolutionary "consciousness could only be brought to them [the workers] from without," that is, from the revolutionary intellectual (Lenin [1902] 1943, 40) who normally has the reserves to forego short-term advantage.

The labor transaction, like other transactions, requires a withholding capability on the part of the buyer and seller to make bargaining possible. Without the ability to withhold, neither side has any incentive to bargain, which really amounts to a bilateral (at least) resolution of what it had previously been able to do unilaterally. Accordingly, collective bargaining over the price of labor and other terms requires that the union be able to mount a sufficient threat to cause management to accept bilateral resolution of the terms of employment and that the employer be able to say no to union demands—or that both sides be able to make credible threats to these effects. The ability of each side to withhold something of importance to the other is the first, if not always the sufficient, condition of bargaining.

There is no direct management analogue to the strike, although the lockout is so perceived. Actually, the employer need not resort to the lockout to have his way. Since the worker cannot change the terms of employment unilaterally and the employer's consent is always required to make any change operative, all the employer needs to do is to say no in order to oppose union demands. Therefore, the initiative to withhold always has to come from the union and/or a group of workers.

A secondary purpose of the strike is rank-and-file morale. As a shared, intense experience it brings leaders and members closer together and momentarily submerges internal divisions. For that moment at least, the rank and file is completely behind the union.

The strike is also useful in bringing the rank and file to the realization that demands represent costs to them as well as to the employer, and the greater the demands the greater the costs. This is the self-disciplining function which the strike (or, more often, its threat) performs. It is this function of the strike which the union leadership has in mind when it calls for a strike even when it knows that a strike could cost more than it is worth. The strike is, therefore, important as a function as well as a right.

Unions rely on three classes of successive sanctions as bargaining leverage: (1) withholding of labor, (2) withholding of demand for product or service, and in rare circumstances (3) direct action against the physical instruments of production and/or the people who man them. The strike is the most common form of withholding labor. A "primary" strike in American usage withholds labor from the employer who is a direct party to the dispute. A secondary strike withholds labor from an employer who is not directly involved in the dispute but who, in varying degrees, is related to the employer who is.

The secondary strike, better known as the "secondary boycott," is the trickiest branch of American labor law. Without implying a definitive reading of the law it is sufficient for present purposes to single out as major examples of the secondary strike (1) withholding the labor of employees of *another* employer who work side by side with employees of the struck employer, as in the building trades, and (2) withholding the labor of employees of another employer who does business with the struck employer. The specific acts of withholding in this latter category may consist of either a refusal to handle struck goods or to go through another union's picket line. The law turns on the definitions of "employer" and of "ally."

There are strikes which are primary in that labor is withheld from the employer directly involved in the dispute, but that is not their real purpose. Their real purpose is to pressure a third party whose consent is somehow a condition of the employer's acceptance of union demands. An example has been the strike against an employer who cannot increase wages without government consent to increase prices. This sort of strike is really directed against the government. In a variant, a strike in an essential enterprise, commonly in the public sector, aims to inflict enough public inconvenience and hardship to make it difficult for the employer to keep resisting union demands. It is part of the union's calculation to cause the maximum inconvenience and disruptions (see Dunlop 1967, 109–10; Chamberlain 1967, 607).

To cut its costs of striking the union may practice more restricted forms of withholding labor, like the wildcat strike, the slowdown, or the refusal to work overtime. These are, so to speak, "mini-strikes" which achieve the same end as longer withholding actions but at lower costs to the union.

A consumer boycott encourages the withholding of *demand* for the product or service produced by a struck employer. The union resorts to the boycott when a strike appears to be losing its effectiveness in hurting the struck employer.

A picket line usually accompanies the withholding action, whether it is primary or secondary. The pickets, by carrying signs, announce the existence of a strike and try to deter access to the struck premises. The picket line is usually a symbolic deterrent, but it occasionally turns violent.

Direct action deters operation of a struck plant by physical force. The picket line can sometimes turn into a form of direct action when an attempt is made to bring workers across a picket line and pickets resist. The sit-down strikes of the 1930s by auto and rubber workers represented direct action too, since the purpose was to render the struck plant physically inoperable. Sabotage —the classic form of direct action associated with the Industrial Workers of the World (IWW) in the early decades of the twentieth century—is rarely resorted to today. When used, it is more of a symbolic act aimed against a piece of the employer's property than against a whole plant. In any event, sabotage is a sanction of last resort when all other, less drastic sanctions have failed to hurt the employer sufficiently to bring him to terms.

The struck employer typically intends to resume the relationship after the strike. He deliberately chooses not to "break" the picket line or engage in other action which would embitter the post-strike atmosphere. Most employers, therefore, suspend production during the strike as a matter of course rather than to risk picket-line violence and ill-feeling for a long time afterward. Strikes have become routinized; each side looks at the withholding action simply as a necessary part of the bargaining exercise.

The strike has not withered away with the maturing of industrial relations, as some had predicted. To be sure, there has been a normalizing tendency in the conduct of strikes, and some issues which were strike issues are now resolved by some legalized due process, including the complex of dispute resolution procedures in the public sector. But the strike, however its shapes and forms change, is still integral to collective bargaining. There is a critical core element about the strike which, so far, seems to be proof against replacement or rationalization. The persistence of the strike in the public sector, where it is illegal, is indicative of the essential purpose which it seems to serve.

A substantial analytic literature has been devoted to the causes of strikes, and two types of explanations have emerged. One locates the strike-prone element in the character of the workers and their jobs. According to this interpretation, for example, cohesive groups of workers working in self-contained, isolated environments on tough jobs—as in the coal, maritime, and construction industries—are likely to be more strike prone. Or, from another standpoint, "alienated," unhappy workers working on emotionally unrewarding jobs are likely to be more strike prone. The other type of explanation stresses external influences: for example, the movement of real wages, unemployment, and the business cycle. Almost all of the explanations are consistent with the probability that workers are less likely to strike in bad times when their bargaining power is weak, and that employers are more likely to settle than take a strike when business is good. Furthermore, workers are more inclined to strike when they have reason to anticipate attrition of their real wage position (see Kaufman 1982, 473–90).

Waves of strike activity are shaped by tendencies in the industrial relations scene at large; specifically: (1) the strikes of desperation against wage cuts in the late 1920s and pre–New Deal 1930s; (2) the strikes for union recognition accompanying the great wave of organizing during the New Deal 1930s; (3) the ebbing of strikes during World War II; (4) the strike upheaval of the immediate postwar period; (5) the strike decline in the *post*-postwar era; (6) the strike resurgence, marking the compression of real wages during the long inflation of the late 1960s and the "stagfla-tion" of the 1970s; (7) the ebbing of strikes in the recession-de-pressions of the 1980s.

The important qualitative change in the strike in the private sec-tor is that it is no longer the highly charged struggle of the 1930s and before. The strike has been normalized and is symbiotically related to an end, the end being conclusion of an agreement. The strike is, therefore, no longer an overriding end in itself, or the breaking of a strike, a holy cause. It now represents the same kind of withholding option which all buyers and sellers have to have at their disposal to make their bargaining credible.

The parties try to avoid or to minimize strikes if other means are available to resolve differences. Escalator clauses, periodic produc-tivity allowances, and other automatic adjustments represent reso-lution of differences by formula instead of by strike ordeal. Grievance arbitration and long-term contracts and interest arbi-tration and other impasse procedures in the public sector represent "rational" alternatives to the strike.

Government has stepped in to resolve by rule of law what would otherwise be strikeable issues: NLRB elections are available to re-solve questions of union representation and recognition; the bar-gainability of certain contract terms is now settled by law rather than by strike power; mediation services are available to bridge communications gaps between the parties.

Even the conduct of the strike has become routinized. Violence is rare because private sector management accepts the strike as tantamount to plant shutdown. But violence—or direct action, as we have called it—does erupt from time to time. If violence is not mindless, it is designed to shut down an operation after other sanc-tions have failed, or as a method by which one union intimidates another in interunion or union-nonunion rivalry. When the vio-lence is mindless, it expresses rage, frustration, bitterness because the union has been unable to shake the employer's resistance.

Some public sector strikes—by police, fire fighters, hospital, sanitation, or transport workers—do become highly charged strug-gles. Unlike private sector strikes, where the costs are borne by the parties directly involved—employees and employers—the costs of strikes in the public security services are borne mostly by the users of these services. Indeed, strikes of this sort are aimed at creating a crisis serious enough to force the public management to back down in order to preserve the public order. It is not unknown for the public authority to collude with the union in creating an emergency that will force the legislature or a governor to act. As John Dunlop and Derek Bok have noted, the public sector union "can seldom hope to generate much pressure by making the government sustain economic losses. Instead, the strike succeeds, if at all, by inconveniencing the public enough to bring grass roots pressure to bear on elected officials. In this sense, an effective strike by government employees tends inherently to be harmful to the public" (Bok and Dunlop 1970, 335).

Union political action is supplementary—and perhaps is in the process of becoming complementary—to collective bargaining. Political action is also a species of bargaining. Collective bargaining rests on the sanction of withholding labor from the employer; political action, by contrast, rests on withholding (or offering) material and moral support to candidates as a quid pro quo for the candidates' support of union policies.

Because political action is mostly tied to collective bargaining, it has fundamentally the same ends: that is, price and power. Specific union purposes in political action include:

1. The diffusion of union wage standards in the nonunion sector via minimum and prevailing wage laws to lessen low-wage competition;
2. Income redistribution via income transfer programs (social security) and "progressive taxation," etc.;
3. Regulation of labor supply and demand conditions, including the quality of labor, to reenforce union bargaining positions (examples: the support of full employment policies, industry subsidies, or, most recently, protectionist measures to prevent impairment of domestic markets and therefore attrition of union positions, as in steel, autos, textiles and apparel);
4. Strengthening union institutional power, or opposing its weakening (examples: support of the Labor Reform Bill of 1978 or opposition to the Taft-Hartley law).

In periods of expansion unions tend to take a broader view of their interests, not by abandoning group self-interest but by perceiving the relevance of group self-interest to broader national and international policy. In a couple of generations the trade union movement has moved from preoccupation with anti-union measures like the labor injunction toward major emphasis on full employment and social policy. But in the wake of the recessions and political setbacks of the 1980s union public policy stands have taken on a more defensive accent.

The methods of political action are electoral activity and lobbying. Electoral activity includes (1) organizing union influence within the two established political parties, but mostly within the Democratic Party; (2) money, manpower, and morale in support of sympathetic candidates; (3) membership education and propaganda; and (4) getting out the vote. Lobbying includes pressure for favorable or against unfavorable legislative action, and monitoring the enforcement of existing laws, including grass roots pressure. An organizational network engages in such activities as propaganda, education and training, lobbying, registration campaigns, campaign financing and manning, and polling surveys. Trade unionists show up in caucuses at political conventions, as political insiders within the parties, and as candidates and officeholders.

The labor movement's political action is decentralized, following in this respect the decentralized character of the total movement and of the political system in which the unions must function. The political and legislative line of the AFL-CIO as a federation has no binding force on affiliates, and, in fact, the political positions of the affiliates do frequently run counter to the federation's—and to each other's—positions at various times. The threat of Reaganism as perceived by the unions is spurring them toward a more centralized and planned political strategy.

With respect to price and power both in collective bargaining and political action, there is a concomitant goal which might be called social justice or social unionism. All labor movements, including the American, had their origins in, and have an historic association with, social reform and socialist causes. Something of that social justice impulse is, in varying degrees, embodied in the

idea of a labor *movement*—that is, there is a spirit of common purpose that transcends group egoism, commonly called solidarity.

Lacking by now a specific socialist motivation, American social
justice unionism *in practice* is not in opposition to "business
unionism," but an extension of it. When the price of labor takes
the form, for example, of a guaranteed annual wage, a comprehensive health and pension program, and a paid four-week
vacation, and correspondingly, when political and legislative goals
give the highest priority to full employment and social policy, business unionism may be perceived to have fused into social justice.
That is, the union is negotiating via collective bargaining and
politics not only out of narrow self-interest to enhance the price of
a given unit of labor; it is asserting the more solidaristic aim of
negotiating the long-run costs of human maintenance.

Social justice is served when the union seeks power on the job
for the heretofore powerless, low-paid, ethnic minorities. It is important to understand that in the union's self-image it is more than
a labor "marketing" organization—although it has to be that,
whatever else it is. An extra margin in union collective bargaining
and political demands represents social justice or solidarism with
the working class as a whole.

Political action in the United States is tending to take on the attributes of a sub-labor party: as Lane Kirkland has said, "We
have succeeded in building a machinery of our own in terms of
working with our constituency and with related constituencies, independent of the structure of either political party" (Kirkland
1976, 5). There are, however, several important respects in which
this American labor subparty falls short of the West European full-
fledged labor party model. The American labor movement lacks
electoral instruments of its own. American trade union political action is marked, therefore, by an absence of a labor or socialist
ideology and the institutional bonds and loyalties that mark
party–trade union relationships in Western Europe.

The socialist-oriented trade unions of Western Europe are not
unlike the American unions in that they, too, become a special interest group even within their own parties, as against the middle-
class intellectual leadership, on such questions as wage repression.
"Trade unions and political parties perform quite distinct func-

tions," a leader of the British Trades Union Congress has said, "and when the Labor Party is in power, these are divergent functions as well" (TUC 1966, 56).

The relative weight and significance given to trade union politics and legislative and electoral means varies within a union, by types of unions, and according to the environments in which unions find themselves. Industrial unionism favors political action that is more broadly defined, more broadly based, and more programmatic. This is because industrial unionism's environment—automobiles, steel, rubber, etc.—is in the center of the economy, cutting through virtually every economic and social issue. Indeed, industrial unionism owes its existence to an act of public policy. Craft unionism leans toward more limited "pressure group" political action. The craft union, seeking limited objectives—that is, increasing jobs in its trade or limiting the supply of entrants to a particular craft—is more likely to be concerned with local and state politics. It is also more likely to collaborate with Republicans. For unions in public service, in publicly regulated enterprise, and in military-related enterprise—that is, in those situations where government is an employer, or an employer once-removed—political bargaining carries greater weight than collective bargaining. But unions, whether craft or industrial, private sector or public sector, will pursue their political action wherever job preservation takes them, as witness the protectionist directions in which the heretofore "free trade" industrial unions have recently been forced to go.

Bargaining effectiveness has required union governance to accommodate to its employer's market, the employer's technology, political action, internal union sectionalism, and businesslike administration. But the logic of bargaining effectiveness does not always prevail. Tradition and jobs sometimes displace effectiveness.

There are five levels of union government. The shop level is more or less coextensive with the plant work society. Its main function is to speak for its constituency in the day-to-day aspects of the employment relationship, including grievances. One or more shop units commonly make up a local union. The local union is the nuclear unit of formal union government with the authority, granted to it by the national union, to tax and discipline its members and to enter into formal agreements with management.

The intermediate body is most commonly an association of local unions created to reduce rivalry in dealing with common employers and to coordinate the interests of several local unions in areas of common interest. This body—as "joint council" or "district council"—combines, coordinates, and, not infrequently, displaces the collective bargaining function of local unions in the large city, metropolitan area, or region. The intermediate-level organization arose to take over functions of otherwise competing units of the same national. Other typical forms of the intermediate body include the corporation council or industry council, which brings together locals of the same national dealing with a common industry or common employer. The occupational council or department, as in the white-collar council or skilled workers council, is the vehicle which brings together locals with a common craft constituency. The fourth level, the national union, occupies the kingpin position in American trade union government and is the ultimate source of constitutional authority for the subordinate bodies. It is typically the decisive influence in collective bargaining, the core function of American trade unionism. Unions are government-like associations with written constitutions, organs to carry out the terms of their constitutions, effective sanctions to enforce compliance by their members, and due process standards to protect members from arbitrary use of power, the last forced on most unions by the law. Union constitutions vest sovereignty in a popular constituency, either directly through a referendum or a mass meeting or indirectly through a delegate assembly. The constitutions also set out the objects, organs, and functions of the government and lay claim to a jurisdiction or territory.

From the beginning, national unionism has been a calculated undertaking in the coordination of sectional union interests spurred by the nationalization and even internationalization of the markets in which unions function. The rise of the national unions to the commanding position in the network of union government reflects the economies of scale and the expansion of union functions to such a degree that only the national union has had sufficient resources to finance them.

The federation, here equated with the AFL-CIO, is a federal-type association of national unions who are free to affiliate or not to affiliate. The federation includes two types of subfederations: (1) city and state federations composed of federation-affiliated locals in their respective areas, and (2) trade and industrial departments which bring together national unions with a common interest in specific categories of industries.

The merger movement among national unions which started out strong in the wake of the newly unified AFL and CIO turned sluggish a decade later. This caused George Meany to complain "that the responsible officers of many unions who by all logic and common sense should merge might well take a broader view of the union movement as an instrument of progress for working people rather than as an institution devoted to its own perpetuation for the sake of sentiment and tradition." The Bureau of Labor Statistics reports that "merger activity has been sustained at a high level since 1968" (USBLS 1980, 53).

The main problem in union governance is the poor adjustment between fragmented bargaining structures and the centralizing tendencies in the employers with whom they bargain. By and large this represents a union choice of self-determination over efficiency. Nowhere has this been more evident over the years than in the craft-type structures in construction, printing, air transport, railroads and the public sector. This fragmentation has been a major cause of their troubled industrial relations.

Union fragmentation in these industries and others has made it difficult for the unions to formulate long-term, industrywide strategy instead of the short-run maximizing which they mostly pursue. In addition, craft structures have bred jurisdictional disputes (disputes over which union is entitled to do the work), a particular problem of the building trades but by no means limited to them. Industrial-type unions also clash with one another in representation disputes. Such clashes (over which union shall represent the workers) are commonly resolved by an NLRB representation proceeding.

Except for the craft bargaining structures mentioned previously, inclusive or industrial-type unionism has become the order of the day. But rivalry between groups of workers is not thereby eliminated. The greater inclusiveness of the unit brings with it "pressures for internal equity" (Rehn 1957, 228) initiated by industrial units within predominantly craft unions and by craft, white-collar, and professional employees within predominantly industrial unions. This sectional pressure has been one of the reasons for the establishment of the occupational-type intermediate bodies referred to earlier. For example, the "industrialization" of erstwhile craft unions has spurred the establishment of internal "manufacturing departments." Conversely, specialized occupational departments are organized within the industrial unions for professional and white-collar groups. What the unions are doing in effect, is to create orderly channels through which internal pressure can be asserted.

Tribunals in the federation and several trade and industrial departments chaired by impartial outsiders represent mechanisms to resolve inter- and intra-union disputes over jurisdiction and representation. Tribunals in several national unions function as courts of appeal in disciplinary cases, and in at least one union an independent "ethical practices" committee decides whether officers have been guilty of improper acts.

The most significant development in internal union governance has been the new assertiveness of the rank and file, which can be dated from the early 1960s. This assertiveness has been expressed through a variety of actions: (1) strikes, both authorized and unauthorized, during the life of an agreement; (2) local-issues bargaining under a national agreement; (3) insurgency, frequently successful, against long-established incumbents, as in steel, coal, and the Teamsters; (4) contract rejections and decertifications; and (5) civil rights confrontation on the shop floor and in the local union.

Procedures have been introduced which allow craft units to veto industrial union settlements and permit local issues bargaining. In addition, legal interventions under the Landrum-Griffin and civil rights laws have provided additional protections for protest from below. The net effect has been to decentralize the locus of power in union government and to establish the rank and file as a permanent and active check and balance on union leadership.

If this commentary had been written a generation or so ago,

overcentralized authority in the national union would have been cited as a major problem of union democracy. But "the problem [now] may well have become too much rather than too little 'responsiveness.' " Clark Kerr has said, "One can only be impressed with how quickly trends can be reversed or brought to a stop" (Kerr 1964, xvii).

The scale and complexity of union organization has required it to take on aspects of businesslike management of its affairs. The increasing importance of full-time staff for organizing, servicing, and bargaining is the most prominent example. In some ways the union staff is a bureaucracy. But this bureaucracy, unlike the classical bureaucracy, comes out of the union's ranks, and its tenure is likely to be much less secure than that of Max Weber's bureaucrat. Professionals in law, economics, public relations, health, and communications are common on union staffs, but they have no political role and are not a managerial elite in any sense.

From time to time the character of the union as enterprise requires it to behave like other managements which have to deal with unions and strikes of employees. This apparent anomaly simply proves the point that when the union becomes a kind of business—and there is no avoiding it if it is to be an effective bargaining organization—it has to function like any other business even if, in relationships with management, it seems to function like an *anti*business organization.

# CHAPTER SIX

# Management as a Bargaining Organization

MANAGEMENT AND UNION differ not only in their interests; they differ organizationally. The union is *primarily* a bargaining organization; if it isn't that, it's nothing. By contrast, for management, bargaining with employees is only one—and not always the most important—aspect of the larger management system of cost discipline. Management's response to the union is what this chapter is about.

In good times the union counters management initiative in the direction of the enterprise with a bargaining initiative. In times of adversity, however, management is just as likely to take the bargaining initiative to gain concessions from the union.

Management attempts to avoid unionism if it can. Union avoidance takes both strategic and tactical forms. As strategy, union avoidance means a long-term employment policy which has as one of its goals keeping the union out, whether or not a union threat is imminent. The point of the strategy is simply to offer the employees a better employment bargain than any union can. Union avoidance as a tactic is a series of steps in the face of an imminent union threat.

The strategy of union avoidance is now practiced not only by "those who hate unions," a management spokesman has said, "but by those who have concluded in the most dispassionate of ways that living without a union is a sound business decision" (Pestillo 1979, 234). The mark of the eighties is that union avoidance is being practiced by many managements with a long history of dealing with unions. The ascendant management ideology is "that if the company does its job well, the employees—or at least a large majority of them—will believe that a union is unnecessary"

(Foulkes 1980, 134). By contrast, I could write some twenty-five years ago that "many tough bargainers [among employers] prefer the union to a situation where there is no union. . . . Most of the employers in rubber, basic steel and the automobile industry fall in that category" (Barbash 1956, 210).

In the view of Peter Pestillo (now industrial relations vice-president for Ford but in charge of industrial relations for B. F. Goodrich when he said this; both are union companies) the change in employer attitudes is due to the fact that "today unions just haven't been able to deliver." They have not been able to deliver protection from wage competition either domestically or, more essentially, internationally. Second, unions "have suffered a loss of union leadership because the leaders have been incapable of resisting unreasonable rank and file claims." Third, "the structure extensive unionization tends to impose on a personnel system . . . has proved too unwieldly in today's times" (Pestillo 1979, 234–35).

Managements which seek to keep unions away have had to institute compensatory policies for "employment security, . . . effective upgrading, training and career development, . . . improved communications, profit sharing or other such equity-participation plans and more sensitive supervisors and managers" (Foulkes 1980, 157). This can be as costly as, or more costly than, dealing with a union (management is "satisficing" rather than maximizing here), but the payoff for management is that it does not have to cope with union power. Management, in this "union substitution" strategy, finds itself doing many of the things which a union does but without having to suffer an active union presence. In effect, management is "buying out" the union impulse of its employees in the interest of greater power and flexibility for itself.

Union avoidance as a range of tactics is indicated in an American Management Association course on preventive labor relations for the nonunion employer. The syllabus covers the following main topics:

How to recognize and resist union organizing early
Judging your company's capability for countering a
union drive

Legal boundaries—how far can you go in resisting
unionization
Positive campaign strategies . . .
How to handle typical organizing incidents
How to build viable election day and post-election
strategies
Practicing preventive labor relations to make unions
unnecessary in your company (AMA 1980)

If the union gains entry, management's objective is to prevent
the expansion of the " 'network of rules' . . . to a point where
[management's] ability to respond to as yet unforeseen problems
and challenges is not too greatly affected.'' The economic objective is to prevent the shifting of ''the real cost of labor too far 'out
of line' '' (McCarthy 1969, 3).

Union encroachment into management territory is a necessary
consequence of the collective bargain. Negotiation of the price of
labor, as we have seen, cannot be separated from the manner in
which labor is to be utilized. This means that the critical employment decisions relating to classification, tenure, and effort—the
composition of labor's price—which had previously been made
unilaterally, become, under collective bargaining, subject to challenge by the union. As distinguished from the informal bargaining
with the work society, union bargaining formalizes the challenge
to management authority and provides a procedure through which
the challenge can function.

The union differs, therefore, from the work society in presenting a more visible challenge to management authority. The work
society bargains but only rarely negotiates: that is, the bargaining
is implicit, but it is unusual for it to be carried on across the table
face to face. Moreover, the results of work society bargaining
never get incorporated into a detailed written agreement, and the
terms of reference are much narrower in scope.

Unions also contain a political dimension which the work society
does not have. Most unions are associated with liberal and, in the
minds of many managers, antibusiness if not antifree enterprise
movements. There is therefore a strong ideological coloration to
the union's demand for the sharing of power. Overall, the union

presence calls attention to the sharing of prerogatives in a way that the work society does not, and—to allude to an earlier point—in a way that management's own tendency toward "power equalization" through human relations does not. Management is not unprepared to share authority, providing it can do so on its own terms.

The theory of management rights rests on the assumption that preservation of its authority or, the corollary, the containment of union power is essential to protect the integrity of management's right to manage. As put by active practitioners on the management side:

> The issue of power in labor relations is the cardinal factor in every contract negotiation. (McMurry 1967, 226)

> Of primary concern to management is clear and strong language setting out its rights and prerogatives. (Marceau 1969, 120–21)

> The struggle for power must automatically be focused [on the management rights clause]. (Ibid., 158)

Over and above efficiency there is undoubtedly a "taste for power" in management's resistance to the union. Curiously enough, there is some evidence that union plants are more productive and experience lower quit rates (Freeman 1982, 3). The taste for power is seen, for example, in the not uncommon employer threat to close the plant before he lets the union tell him how to run his business. For many employers it may be that the real hurt in the relationship with the union is in the sharing of "managerial," i.e. power, prerogatives more than in sharing "market," i.e. price, prerogatives. Managements are "readier to negotiate with employees about the terms on which they are to be hired than about how they are utilized and deployed once they have been hired" (Fox 1971, 158). When the luster of economic advancement diminishes, it is the joy of power (or self-actualization, if you like) which really makes managers' jobs interesting.

Like unions, managements resort to the strategies of internal bargaining, collective bargaining, and public policy bargaining. Also like the union, internal bargaining is made necessary by the complexity and scale of the management organization. The "lower participants" in the management structure—foremen, for example—being closer to the rank and file may be more inclined to tolerate "rule-breaking" down below (Fox 1971, 88) in the interests of getting along. Just as the steward is, in a sense, a mediator between his constituents and his management, so lower management also partakes of a mediating role but in reverse. The point has been insistently made that the foreman's status has been "undermined by a proliferation of managerial specialists, by the growth of hierarchy and by new channels of communication between higher management and his work-group subordinates which often by-pass him altogether" (ibid., 85).

Rather than being loyal to the company, managers become committed to their "specialized function and ideology" (ibid., 87), and this causes them to view union demands in diverging ways.

> One finds members of a line faction cooperating with a staff group to defeat union demands. And simultaneously one might find line executives opposing efforts of the same staff to change some production method. Or again circumstantial compulsions may lead line chiefs to cooperate with union officers to exploit a piece rate system set up by the industrial engineers, while some members of the union confidentially agree with the engineers on a point of incentive pay defeating the interests of other union members and the aims of line executives. (Dalton 1959, 19–20)

Internal bargaining, a concept first illuminated by Walton and McKersie (1965, 281–351), within management differs from union internal bargaining in that it is mainly underground and largely unstructured in form and process. Moreover, pressure groups within management are more likely to achieve unity—or for that matter, to be forced into it—at the point of bargaining with the union. In the public sector internal differences are built into the management structure by the doctrine of the separation of powers, so that who the operative employer is depends on the function being exercised.

If collective bargaining and the union come to pass, the unionized company is likely to come to terms with the collective bargaining game. This means accepting the union as the employees' spokesman, playing the game of collective bargaining within its broad rules and probably, once collective bargaining has been initiated, finding that it is less costly to deal with the union than to wage permanent warfare against it.

The sanctions available to management in containing and resisting union bargaining demands are first and primarily the ability to withhold demand for union labor. Management can subcontract the work formerly performed by its own employees. It can reject union demands and inflict the costs of a strike on the union and its members; it can lock out the employees. Management can accept the inevitability of a strike but minimize its costs by prestrike stockpiling and strike insurance. Most often the withholding of demand for labor is temporary until agreement is reached, but management can withhold demand permanently by replacing strikers, contracting out, and, as a last resort, closing or relocating the plant.

Management counterstrike strategy seems to have evolved from the strikebreaking and anti-unionism of the 1930s to "taking a strike" and, if necessary, a long strike. Taking a long strike means, as a practical matter, increasing the risks of striking to the strikers by withholding agreement and prolonging the strike at some point beyond the tolerable margin of the strikers' staying power. At the same time, the employer may act to cut his own risks through strike insurance, automated operations, prestrike overtime, stockpiling, relocation of production, and imports. Over the longer term, the employer, in concert with other employers, may carry on campaigns against welfare, food stamps, and unemployment compensation for strikers.

The counterstrategy of the long strike is currently evident in the public sector, where fiscal retrenchment has emboldened public managements to pursue a harder line. This hard line has included strike replacements, injunctions, and fines, and has been particularly noticeable in several teachers' strikes. The strikebreaking strategy recurs from time to time, the most thoroughgoing case being the dismissal of strikers in the air controllers' strike of 1981.

Once in a while there is a reversion to earlier confrontations in which employers perceive the strike as not only an economic but also an ideological conflict. The West Coast growers undoubtedly saw their struggle with Chavez's farmworkers in such a light. The Kohlers must also have seen their decades-long conflict with the UAW in this way. But causes have a way of dissipating their ideology and fervor. The farmworkers seem on their way toward normalizing collective bargaining with the growers. The UAW and Kohler have been engaged in an amicable collective bargaining relationship for more than a decade now.

In a second order of sanctions, management comes to terms with the union but thereafter seeks to cut the costs of recognition. It may install more economical methods of labor utilization; it may toughen its grievance handling; or it may seek to exclude certain terms of employment from bargaining by professionalizing the technique, as in Scientific Management.

There is what might be called the "captive union" tactic, which weakens union power not by attrition but by "kindness." In this tactic the employer captures the union in a much more sophisticated way than by controlling the union mechanism, as in the old pre-Wagner company unionism. Management dampens union militancy by concessions which it does not have to make or by initiating concessions which would have to be made eventually anyway. What management is buying is pliability, with the purpose of eroding active identification between the employee and the union. In such circumstances, union leadership finds it extremely difficult to get the support of the membership for striking, and much of its cutting edge as a fighting institution is dulled, and in some instances, destroyed (Barbash 1956, 211).

Cooptation can evolve into collusion. In collusion, employers in a local market negotiate unduly favorable terms of employment in return for which the union undertakes to deny new firms access to a labor supply.

Captive management is the opposite of the coopted or captive union—also typically a local-market phenomenon. Here the union enforces its power and authority with such a strong and occasionally violent hand that the employer, perforce, gives the union anything it wants.

There are employers who favor a strong union because it is more efficient to deal with than a weak union. The employer recognizes that the "lack of strong and secure union leadership backed up by the union rank and file [makes] bargaining more time-consuming and difficult" (Smith 1959, 18). In this approach a strong union need not necessarily yield less economical results because the leaders feel secure enough to confront powerful factions with the dysfunctional consequences of their demands. Accordingly,

> Management can help strengthen the position of the more promising fairminded steward with his member by trying wherever possible to give him something to take back to him. . . . Too many noes will undermine the position of the steward who must transmit them to his members. . . . It pays dividends in sound relationships for management to recognize the steward's job as typically a thankless one and to help him build up his prestige and effectiveness. (Selekman 1947, 65–67 passim)

Once managements are in collective bargaining, they may elect to cut the costs of union dealing by a variant on problem solving, sometimes also called cooperative, collaborative, or integrative bargaining, or quality of working life. I call it rational persuasion. The assumption is that there are labor problems that can be resolved with advantage, or with the least disadvantage, to *both* sides through rational examination rather than by each side inflicting punishment on the other. This is problem solving because the objective is not to enhance or diminish the position of one side against the other but to deal with a difficult situation. A functioning grievance procedure is probably the most pervasive example of acceptable problem solving in collective bargaining. GM, which has been reexamining its industrial relations philosophy in recent times, has been heard to voice such sentiments as the following:

> An awareness and understanding of the concerns and needs of others, and willingness to be more responsive to these concerns and needs. (Fuller 1980, 37)

> A development of mutual trust and mutual respect for the needs of the business as well as for the concerns of the employes. Above all else, this cooperation must be mutual and sincere. . . . A growth in the long-range trend for management and union to jointly initiate activities that will improve the work environment. (GM 1978, n.p.)

The adversity of the 1980s has brought about a few other management conversions out of necessity, but it is too early to tell whether the mutual trust ideology will take permanently when and if normality returns.

Like unions, managements also utilize a public strategy in bargaining, seeking to reenforce their cost and power objectives by opposition to or support of legislation and administrative rulings. Lobbying, political action committees, and political contributions are the means. Historically, business resorted to the courts to avoid collective bargaining. After the Wagner Act, employers' main public policy objective was to seek redress of the balance of power in their favor through statutory change, the appointment of sympathetic regulators and office-holders, and the election of sympathetic presidents, governors, and so on.

Policy and professionalization appear to be the dominant forces shaping the development of management as a collective bargaining organization. Increasingly, management policy is guided more by systematic analysis and rules than by opportunism and ideology. There is even something which may be called a social responsibility ethic, analogous to the union's "social justice." Professionalism means that collective bargaining is administered by a corps of full-time staff trained for their jobs in schools of business and nurtured by an industrial relations community of consultants, professional associations, and university research. A large part of the movement toward policy and professionalization represents the shock effect of unionism and collective bargaining, and another part, the long-run bent of American enterprise toward the science of management. Yet this does not mean, by a long shot, that the more visceral styles are altogether in the past.

Public sector management differs from its counterpart in the private sector at several critical points. First, there is no market for public goods which communicates clear and unmistakable signals as to how far management (and unions too, for that matter) may safely go in negotiations without impairing its competitive position. Second, management's efficiency or cost discipline interests are necessarily constricted by political considerations: the bottom line is not all. Third, there is no unified employer authority. Depending on the circumstances, the employer is variously the executive, the legislature—local or statewide—or a civil service commission, all of which makes it possible for the union to play one face of the employer or management against another.

In general terms, management as a bargaining organization pursues a hard or a soft line. The soft line operates in an expansionary climate when a high level of demand is virtually assured at any price. The hard line is more likely to be found in the climate of recession and contraction. The 1980 recessions mark the heaviest offensive yet against union power since the 1930s, with the difference that in the thirties the offensive took the form of open confrontation; in the eighties the management offensive is by negotiation.

# CHAPTER SEVEN

# The Collective Bargaining Interaction

THIS CHAPTER examines collective bargaining as an interaction process between management and workers represented in a union and normally resolved by a collective agreement.

Collective bargaining is only one point, albeit a major point, along a continuum of diverse modes of joint dealing between workers and employers. At one end—the negation of joint dealing—is management unilateralism in which the right and power to make decisions is vested solely in management. At the other pole is workers' control.

At an interval along the way is human relations and its later variants. Human relations is still management in charge but with greater responsiveness to the needs of the lower participants in the enterprise. Consultation, at a still further remove, is West European usage and generally represents a type of formalized joint dealing in which the workers have a right to be informed, to question proposed management policies, and to get a response; but the eventual decision is made by management and is not contingent on negotiation with the workers' side. The American analogue is "meet and confer," found in some public sector statutes.

In the collective bargaining type of joint dealing, decisions relating to the terms of employment are contingent on a negotiated agreement with an appropriate union. Codetermination—German in origin and setting—is, in its fullest development, the right of the workers' representatives to join with top management in the making of decisions in a predefined area, whether in the employment area or not. (In practice, codetermination has been mostly confined to the employment terms.) Industrial democracy also means codecisionmaking but, in the contemporary context, on, or at least closer to, the shop floor. Collective bargaining that comes close to codetermination or industrial democracy may occur in the American public sector; teachers may be a case in point. A kind of limited codetermination has emerged in the United States, most notably between Chrysler and the UAW, as a crisis response.

Craft unions come close to workers' control, in effect if not in ideology, when the employer either acquiesces in the union's terms or goes out of business. In the recent hard times, building trades employers have been able to refine the option of going nonunion. Craft unions are normally powerful enough to incorporate major terms of employment in their internal rules rather than to have to negotiate them in collective bargaining. Full-fledged workers' control—syndicalism in an earlier time—is the negation of joint dealing on the workers' side and exists nowhere as a working arrangement, although it is the subject of considerable discussion.

Collective bargaining in the United States is a continuous process in which unions, as designated representatives of workers in specified units, and the appropriate public or private managements negotiate the terms of employment. The parties complement their collective bargaining with supporting activities in politics and public policy. The plan of this chapter is to elaborate on the key terms in this definition.

"Unit" describes the employment territory—occupation, craft, department, multiplant, multiemployer, public jurisdiction, etc., or combinations thereof—to which a particular collective bargaining relationship applies. The bargaining unit is commonly established in a representation proceeding conducted by the National Labor Relations Board or a similar agency. But the unit established for representation need not be the same as the units for organizing, negotiation, or grievance handling, which are shaped by the exigencies of each situation.

The terms of employment which the parties bargain about are, fundamentally: (1) the price of labor, e.g., wages, supplements, methods of wage determination, wage structures; (2) the implementing rules which define how the labor is to be utilized (which, as we have seen, give meaning to the price) including hours, work practices, job classifications, and the effort input; (3) individual job rights, e.g., seniority, discharge for cause; (4) the rights of union and management in the bargaining relationship—for the union, the union shop, checkoff, and variations, and for the employer the right of management to manage; (5) the enforcement, interpretation, and administration of the agreement, including the resolution of grievances and bargaining structures. But the stakes of collective bargaining, we may say, come down basically to price and power.

The evolution of the wage rate into a complex compensation structure has become the main new price-of-labor ground plowed by collective bargaining. Health insurance, pensions, paid holidays and vacations, and the technical methods of wage determination are the prominent components of that structure.

In contrast with the upward and onward mood of the postwar generation, bargaining since the late seventies has taken place against the pessimistic economics of recession and, for some industries, depression. Unions are now more concerned with holding their own than with innovating. As this is being written, wage concessions have become the order of the day across almost the entire bargaining front. The mass unemployment and layoffs of recession have pushed job security to the fore once again. Even such union powerhouses as the construction unions, the Teamsters, and the printing trades have found it necessary to ease their rules in order to stanch the flow of employers into the nonunion sector.

Collective bargaining, as we have observed, is normally integrated with internal bargaining and political bargaining. In internal bargaining, as Walton and McKersie have instructed us in their classic work (1965), it is necessary for each of the parties to bargain out their positions *within* their respective organizations before they can bargain with each other. Internal bargaining on the management side is most marked in the public sector, where the separation of power inherent in constitutional government creates several frequently competing voices, each purporting to speak in behalf of some aspect of the employer-management interest. On the union side, internal bargaining is most marked in the industrial unions because of the greater diversity of their constituencies. The collective bargaining of public employees involves bargaining with public administrators and politicians. Political bargaining represents a reenforcement of the parties' bargaining interests through public policy.

To recapitulate, bargaining requires sanctions which, by promise of benefit, threat of withholding, rational persuasion, and direct action, induce the other side to agree and compromise. The strike is the union's major sanction even if, as in the public sector, it is mainly illegal. On occasion the strike is backed up by consumer boycotts—which is the collective withholding of product demand—and by direct action. Withholding of employment is the employer's major sanction. Not all sanctions are intended to disadvantage the other side. Positive sanctions or promise of benefit may also induce the parties to agree. Standardization of labor costs, the improvement of the employer's product market position (i.e., the union label), and orderly conflict resolution on the shop floor (i.e., the grievance procedure) serve the interests of both parties.

The negotiating table is figuratively and literally the forum in which parties face each other in the making of the bargain. Negotiation, normally face to face or through mediation, allows the proclaimed positions of the parties to be modified through continuous feedback and exchange of information.

While negotiation is part of bargaining, not all bargaining involves negotiation. That is to say, terms and sanctions can be communicated without face-to-face negotiation and without, of course, the opportunity for instant feedback offered by face-to-face negotiation. Subordinate bargains including, most importantly, grievance processing are also part of the negotiation process.

Negotiation is distinguished from confrontation. Confrontation is a mode of bargaining, but the "fac[ing] in hostility or defiance" that characterizes confrontation makes more difficult, if not impossible, "the game of discovering what the other party really [is] after, its irreducible minimum, and its genuine demands," which is what negotiation is about (Chamberlain and Kuhn 1965, 55). Negotiation is also to be distinguished from a sequence of unilateral actions, as illustrated in the early bargaining between International Harvester and the Molders union: "One side or the other opened 'bargaining' by unilateral action: the employer generally by effecting a wage cut, the union by presenting a citywide ultimatum to all foundry employers calling for a wage increase by a certain date. Managements that failed to comply were generally struck, although compromises were sometimes achieved'' (Ozanne 1967, 5–6).

Collective bargaining, especially the negotiation part of it, is a game frequently played for its own sake as well as for the price and power values it is supposed to advance. The negotiation ritual operates according to well-understood rules and roles which are disregarded at the peril of disorienting the players.

The setting for the negotiation game is a rectangular table (never a round table or no table) with the antagonists physically confronting one another. It is always *de rigeur* for the parties to *demand* (or to reject outright). To request, ask, urge, or implore is a sign of weakness and indecision and must never be communicated directly. Each side must, at first, demand much more than it expects to get, and the other side must, at first, concede nothing or concede much less than it is likely to later. If one side makes a concession, it will negotiate for a concession in return. The tradeoff need not be in the same area of negotiation.

Because the parties are not fools, they have developed ways of communicating their realistic expectations. But this straightforward communication has to take place *away* from the visible bargaining table, either through a mediator, or when the principal negotiators from each side retreat to another venue to carry on the ''real negotiations'' less histrionically.

The real negotiations are carried on away from the goldfish bowl so as not to violate the macho spirit obligatory in the public negotiations. Under the macho rule no player can even intimate that the resolve of his side is something less than granitic. Nor is it in the spirit of things to concede weaknesses in one's own position or acknowledge the strong points in the position of the other side.

The theatrical behavior and the strong talk indulged in by each side are directed not only at their antagonists. For the union this is a way of communicating to the rank and file that they are not being ''sold out.'' The management bargainers, being in a different kind of political organization—more of a hierarchy, that is—are not under the same pressure to prove their manhood.

Nevertheless, even management cannot afford to show signs of premature acceptance for fear of creating false expectations, or for fear of creating the impression among its stockholders and the business community that it is "giving the store away."

The gamesmanship of the negotiations is only one part of a larger adversary mold into which the whole bargaining relationship is cast. The reality of adversarialism is that the parties do have something to differ about, namely, price and power. These differences are exaggerated, however, to fulfill the expectations of the parties' respective audiences, who see the negotiators as actors playing roles assigned to them by the collective bargaining scenario. There is also a class angle to the labor transaction which most bargainers unconsciously (or sometimes consciously) assimilate into their roles.

Management is the initiating party in the direction of the enterprise. The union mostly reacts. In negotiations these roles are reversed: unions initiate and managements react. Collective bargaining is a union defense against management initiatives in the direction of the enterprise. But in difficult times it is management which is likely to take the bargaining initiative.

Negotiation and bargaining are popularly associated with the process which leads to the written agreement. Negotiation and bargaining of perhaps a different sort are just as important in grievance handling.

Grievance-arbitration is the end point of the collective bargaining procedure which starts out with the negotiation of the written agreement. The agreement sets out the general rules of employment which will prevail for the agreement's duration. It also establishes a grievance procedure for resolving disputes which may arise under its terms. The procedure is most commonly a three-stage, two-sided process capped by impartial arbitration in the event the parties cannot settle the grievance on their own.

Grievance-arbitration represents an alternative to the strike. That is, the union gives up the right to strike over grievances in return for resolution of such grievances by the due process prescribed in the agreement. The strike is still the ultimate sanction in disputes over a *new* contract if the parties cannot agree. In the approved terminology, interest disputes are disputes over the terms of a *new* agreement, and rights disputes are disputes over the interpretation of an *existing* agreement.

As the U.S. Supreme Court put it, grievance-arbitration establishes "a generalized code to govern a myriad of cases which the draftsmen cannot wholly anticipate," and "erect[s] a system of self-government" to apply that code to concrete cases (*USW v. Warrior Gulf and Navigation Co.* 1960). Collective bargaining is, therefore, "constitutive in that it creates new and continuing institutions. . . . Only in part [is] a determinate bargain struck. . . . More important, it is . . . an instrument of industrial self-government" (Selznick 1969, 151; see also Feller 1973, 743). Informal negotiation also goes on *outside* the realm of formal collective bargaining as supervisors and their subordinates continuously negotiate effort values on a one-to-one basis.

The Bureau of Labor Statistics has defined the grievance system as "a means by which an employee, without jeopardizing his job, can express a complaint about his work or working conditions and obtain a fair hearing through progressively higher levels of management" (USBLS 1964, 2). At the end point of the grievance procedure, arbitration settles grievances "through recourse to an impartial third party whose decision is usually final and binding" (USBLS 1965, 5). Certain categories of grievances are sometimes excluded from arbitration—production standards, for example. In that event the union may legally elect to strike during the life of the agreement if the grievance cannot be settled.

Experience seems to have evolved a consensus of the attributes of a well-working grievance-arbitration system:

1. Definiteness. The participants and their roles and functions should be clearly specified.
2. Bilateralism. The system should have parallel paths for grievance processing and review.
3. Exclusivity. Subject only to the grieving employee's right to discuss complaints with the first-line foreman before initiating a grievance, the grievance procedure should be the exclusive route for processing and settling complaints covered by the contract.

4. Appeals procedure. The employee should have the right to appeal to successively higher stages (commonly two) beyond the initial stage.
5. Timeliness. Time limits should be established for processing each stage, on the maxim "justice delayed is justice denied."
6. Decentralization. Inducements for settlement of the disputes in the early stages should be built into the procedure, reserving the upper stages for the more important grievances, and the first stage should not require a written grievance.
7. Differentiation. Grievances involving technical subject matter (time study, insurance, pensions) should be handled separately, and discipline grievances should be handled expeditiously.
8. Impartiality. Fairness can be assured only if the procedure ends with a finding by a third party.
9. Finality. The determination by the third party should dispose of the grievance once and for all, subject only to restricted judicial review.

The cases which grievance-arbitration deals with are thrust up by the continually changing work and market environment in which the enterprise lives. Changes in consumer tastes and technologies, the cycles of recession and expansion, and civil rights tensions all generate a continuous stream of uncertainties. When these combine with idiosyncrasies internal to the plant—cost-cutting management, combative stewards, or aggressive industrial relations directors—tensions become the order of the day. Grievances are, therefore, part of the normal order of things.

The parties' main criticism of grievance-arbitration is that the other side uses it as a pawn in its power-price strategy and not as an impartial judicial procedure to settle grievances on their merits. The rank and file protests the delays, complexities, centralization, and legalisms. The unions complain about the excessive cost of arbitration. For management the delays, complexities, centralization, and legalisms are what it takes to rein in grievance-prone workers, stewards on the make, power-hungry union officials, philosopher-king arbitrators, and liberal-minded judges from undermining management's right to manage and to control costs.

Grievance-arbitration has evolved from the impartial chairman type—cultivated to its highest stage of development in the apparel industries—to arbitration by a judge-like "umpire." The impartial chairman was historically "conciliator, mediator, friend, counselor, and only as a last resort arbitrator" (Fleming 1968, 7). The umpire in mass production is by now a judge who decides what the law is—in this case the private law of the collective agreement—and nothing more. The Supreme Court has said that the arbitrator "does not sit to dispense his own brand of industrial justice" (quoted in Prasow and Peters 1970, 275).

An agreement can set forth only the broad rules for determining the price of labor and the related conditions of sale (See Flanders 1968, 1–26). Only in subsequent shop (or office) floor transactions are the rules translated into a specific price for specific work. This is finally where the individual work bargains are consummated.

The grievance-arbitration system does not really monitor all labor transactions. Only a very small proportion of management's unilateral decisions are protested by workers, and an even smaller number get filtered through to grievance-arbitration. The reasons for this high selectivity are many. To begin with, in the overwhelming majority of management decisions there isn't all that much to complain about. Too, groups and individuals vary widely in their ability to protest. Strategically weak groups or individuals will condone seeming violations of the agreement, perhaps because they fear reprisal otherwise, or because the union representative is weak. Strong groups are frequently in a position to renegotiate informally the terms of the agreement (fractional bargaining) in their favor.

The negotiation of the agreement, even with grievance-arbitration, does not really work out to a *joint* decision-making process between equals in any operational sense. Management still "retains the right to act" on its own in the first instance (Feller 1973, 737). All the grievance procedure does is to make management authority "conditional" (Kuhn 1967, 263), and then only in a small fraction of disputes. In general, the union rejects true joint decision-making—that is, where the parties make decisions together as equals. Instead, the union prefers to leave the initiatives to management. In this way the union is not saddled with the responsibility for joint decisions which may later give rise to grievances.

The grievance-arbitration system is often something more than simply an instrument of compliance and interpretation. It is also in reality a source of *de novo* rulemaking, continuously extending the organic agreement, sometimes even beyond the limits contemplated by the parties, just as the judiciary does not simply interpret the law but also makes new law.

For the most part, grievance-arbitration of the kind discussed here functions in the factory or industrial union setting. Grievance disposal in the crafts is much less complicated. In the building or printing trades, for example, grievances are usually handled unilaterally by the business agent. By contrast with the factory agreement the craft agreement is a simple document. Administration of the agreement is minimal "because there is little to administer. . . . The absence of a grievance procedure is an indication that the determination of compliance or noncompliance with the negotiated scale is a union function and the enforcement mechanism is the one traditional to the trade agreement relationship: the withdrawal of labor'' (Cox 1973, 733).

The grievance-arbitration procedure serves the interests of both sides sufficiently to give both unions and managements a stake in preserving it, although for different reasons. Management of large-scale industry perceives several positive values in the grievance system:

1. The grievance mechanism represents a relatively open channel of communications for labor problems, largely unencumbered by the hindrances of hierarchy. The traditional unilateral systems, even with the best of intentions, communicate mostly what the upper hierarchy likes to hear. The grievance channel tells management much of what it would not otherwise hear about its labor problems, and quite possibly what it would rather *not* hear.
2. The graduated character of the grievance procedure permits large-scale management in effect "to review the action of its lower levels and determine whether that action is in accordance

with the rules. . . . The function of appeal is not simply to obtain an independent judgment; rather its purpose is to bring into play the authority inherent in the hierarchical structure'' (Feller 1973, 743).

3. The grievance procedure permits management to carry out difficult and unpleasant personnel actions like layoffs and discharges, and to contain the discontent which would otherwise follow.

For the union the grievance system legitimizes an active and continuing shop-floor presence which builds institutional loyalty, broadens the base of union participation, and demonstrates the day-to-day usefulness of the union to the rank and file—something which the relatively remote negotiation of the agreement every two or three years does not normally do as well. It is less costly and much less disruptive than striking over every disagreement.

The grievance system is the most valuable part of unionism for the rank-and-file member because it makes possible (1) ''gripes'' and grievances without fear of serious reprisal, (2) personal participation in matters which affect the work, and (3) recourse to the counsel and advocacy of the union leadership in arguing the grievance.

Unions and workers on one side and managements on the other thus have a congruent if not always identical interest in maintaining the grievance-arbitration system at the same time that they pursue adversarial power-price positions in the processing of individual cases.

Unions and managements need not always align against each other in the grievance process. From time to time union leadership and management find themselves informally aligned on the same side against ''irresponsible'' and ''radical'' elements. Union leadership finds that ''responsibility''—that is, working within the spirit of the agreement—is essential if credibility for its more reasonable demands is to be maintained with management. But it is hardly ever politic to say so openly. In the same vein, arbitration serves a scapegoat purpose which permits both sides to acquiesce in unpopular but necessary decisions by blaming the arbitrator.

Structure has to do with how unions and employers organize the collective bargaining relationship internally and with each other. The most worrying problem in structure is the distribution of power within the union as between, to put it broadly, local and national forces. This is what is now at stake, for example, in the Mine Workers Union, where there has been doubt recently as to whether national unionism will be able to survive warring local power centers.

In construction unions "the leapfrogging of settlements" spurred by localism "creates an inflationary bias" (Mills 1980, 74). Many attempts have been made to bring "broader perspectives" to the construction bargaining relationship, the most ambitious being the Ford administration's bill (subsequently vetoed by President Ford) for "a more active national involvement in local bargaining" (ibid., 96).

In less than a generation the locus of the structural problem has shifted from too much power on top to too much power below. What has happened simply is that union democracy has become less important than inflation as a public policy concern. National bargaining structures are favored over local structures because they are better adapted to union responsibility in wage policy.

Inclusive versus exclusive bargaining units is another prominent theme in the structure discussion—rather more in the past than now. The craft versus industrial unionism debate of the 1930s represented its earliest manifestation. The controversy between the construction crafts and the industrial unions over contracting-out is a more modern incarnation, as has been the demand of the skilled workers in the industrial unions for preferred treatment.

Construction and, in a special way, the entertainment industries, including athletics, continue to remain strongholds of craft unionism. The multicraft, projectwide agreements negotiated by the Building and Construction Trades Department attempt to meet the criticism of excessive craft fragmentation in bargaining (Mills 1980, 74–75). In the public sector, however, craft unionism of a sort appears to be the dominant structural type and the one favored by militant elements like the teachers, nurses, police, firefighters, and social workers.

Still another aspect of the inclusive versus exclusive bargaining issue is presented in "coordinated" or "coalition" bargaining, preeminently in GE and Westinghouse. Here the unions seek greater inclusiveness to shore up their weaknesses from union fragmentation in bargaining separately with the megacorporations: "Disunity among the workers . . . powered Boulwarism. . . . Coordinated bargaining [was] the union response to Boulwarism" (Kuhn 1980, 238). But coordinated bargaining is not spreading in the industry. In the public sector it is usually the public *employer* who seeks coordinated bargaining as a shield against union whipsawing.

Multiemployer bargaining is commonly favored by the smaller, relatively weak nonfactory employers to defend themselves against a dominant union in an industry. But even so the evidence in trucking and construction, for example, indicates that the employers' associations are no match for the union. Internal divisions, inadequate financing, and the inexperience of the bargainers defeat association efforts to provide an effective counterweight to the strong union. Apparently, exiting from the union sector altogether is proving to be the more potent weapon in bringing these unions to terms.

The prevailing tendencies in structure are toward diffusion of power. Localized bargaining structures seem to be the "natural" state in the nonfactory environments of trucking and construction. Hoffa's effort to reverse that state by nationalization of the bargaining in over-the-road transport seems to be faltering in the hands of his successors. Reforms in the locally centered construction industry are making some headway, but the center of the power is still in the locals and district councils.

Craft distinctions, another sort of power diffusion, are so deep-rooted in the hospital and health industries as to constitute unbridgeable caste barriers; the same is true in the airlines. The separation-of-powers doctrine inclines public sector bargaining toward fragmented employer authority. Even when one union is in a leading position, as in steel and coal, the forces of internal dispersion of power inhibit the ability of the union to function like a monolith, absent a "strong man" leader.

In a relatively few cases, the influence of an individual leader has made the difference between centralization and decentralization, but these instances are decreasing as dominant personalities like John L. Lewis, Philip Murray, James Hoffa, and (in a somewhat different style) César Chavez become fewer. At this moment only Chavez among the national leaders remains in this stellar category, and even he is facing internal dissension.

Decentralization is the essence of the bargaining structure nationally. There are in the neighborhood of 781,000 separate agreements, not counting health, welfare, and pension supplements (USBLS 1980). Small units dominate in American bargaining organization; most agreements are with single employers and single plant–single employers. But these agreements are not likely to be as influential in setting the general tone of collective bargaining as the relatively small number of key bargains. Collective bargaining on the union side is carried on by more than 200 national unions, including about 75,000 local unions and countless shop committees. Most unions bargain in several industries, and any given industry is likely to have several leading unions. The average national union, which is the linchpin in American union structure, does not have many members, although the majority of union members are found in a relatively few unions.

Power in collective bargaining at the moment seems to be moving both upward and downward. On the up side are such indicators as industrywide negotiations (steel); coordinated bargaining (electrical equipment); multicarrier strike insurance (airlines until recently); coordination of multinational union interests, though short of bargaining (auto, steel, electrical equipment); erratic public policy efforts at wage restraint which make the AFL-CIO a more influential actor in collective bargaining; growth in union membership (USBLS 1980, 53–54); and areawide bargaining in construction.

Indicators of decentralization are the emergence of rank-and-file pressure as a permanent counterweight to leadership; local-issues bargaining (steel, auto); craft self-determination, as in skilled trades and white-collar representation within industrial unions (steel and electrical equipment); insurgent movements (coal, trucking, steel, postal service); the shop-floor politics of race (steel, autos); local government unionism (education, hospitals); and national severance (the separation of Canadian units from U.S. "in-

ternational'' unions). A mark of the changed bargaining environment of the 1980s is the devolution of bargaining structure as management takes advantage of its strengthened position to tailor
structure closer to the individual firm and plant (see Freedman
1982).

The maturing of a bargaining relationship brings about another
sort of decentralization when the parties turn to joint problem-
solving committees both at the shop floor and higher levels. These
committees carry such designations as labor-management cooperation, quality of worklife, quality circles, health and safety,
human relations and health, welfare and pensions (See Siegel and
Weinberg 1982).

The prevailing terms of price and power are in large measure functions of the state of the economy generally and the industry in
which the bargainers find themselves. Unions are obviously in a
stronger position in an expanding economy and industry. At this
writing the condition of the American economy is not favorable to
the enhancement of union price and power objectives. After a half-
century there seems to be in the making a reversal of the bargaining field with the bargaining initiative shifting to management and
away from the unions. Throughout this work and particularly in
this chapter, the new turn of collective bargaining events in the
1980s has been serving as a counterpoint to the generally upward
and onward trend of union influence in our time. Perhaps this is
the place to take a more coherent look at changes which seem to be
looming ahead in collective bargaining. The Roosevelt 1930s
launched a half-century of union ascendancy. Some think that the
Reagan 1980s is beginning to set the stage for an extended period
of union retreat and a realignment in the balance of bargaining
power from unions to business.

The scenario that seems to be unfolding runs, in brief, as follows. Adverse economic circumstances are forcing the unions to
concede the bargaining initiative to management under threats of
plant shutdowns, loss of market, and contracting-out. In this reversal of field it is the union which is now cast in the reacting role.
Management is using its new-found initiative to secure major
wage, rules, and bargaining structure concessions from the

unions. The price the unions are demanding and getting for their acquiescence includes generally a look at the books, job security protection, more say in management decision-making, and the treatment of the wage concessions as deferred obligations subject to later repayment in various forms if circumstances warrant.

The economic adversity which has fueled this turnabout has been in the making for perhaps a decade, but it has taken the recessions of the eighties to bring bargaining to this flash point. These last fifty years or so were, of course, not unfailingly upward for the unions. The upswings have been interrupted from time to time by temporary setbacks, and even at that, all segments of the working population did not share evenly in the forward movement.

The end of union ascendancy has meant a shift in union strategy from the aggressive pursuit of ''more'' to the defense of existing standards, including at times the defense of its own survival. The central fact is that American management no longer takes unions as given in its future calculations; this includes managements with whom the unions thought they had made the case for collective bargaining a long time ago. A large segment of management, it has been observed, holds to the ideology ''that if the company does its job well, the employees—or at least a large majority of them—will believe that a union is unnecessary'' (Foulkes 1980, 134).

The overriding question is whether the long cycle of economic expansion which has underwritten union ascendancy over the last half-century has now come to a halt for the long-term future. Despite the postwar recessions which had periodically interrupted the long expansion, nobody really questioned the vitality of the American economy before. It is the indelible mark of the eighties, not only in the United States but everywhere in the West, that that vitality is being questioned now. The present recession, in this way of thinking, is more than a phase of a business cycle which too shall pass. The feeling abroad in the industrial world is that the West, led by the United States, has lost its forward momentum for a long time to come.

But prophecy can be dangerous. Just about a half-century ago, a renowned academic scholar of industrial relations said:

American trade unionism is slowly being limited in influence by changes which destroy the basis on which it is erected. It is probable that changes in the law have adversely affected unionism. Certainly the growth of large corporations has done so. But no one who carefully follows the fortunes of individual unions can doubt that over and above these influences, the relative decline in the power of American trade unionism is due to occupational changes and to technological revolutions.

. . . It is hazardous to prophesy, but I see no reason to believe that American trade unionism will so revolutionize itself within a short period of time as to become in the next decade a more potent social influence than it has been in the past decade. This is by no means to say that trade unionism in the United States is on its way to insignificance as a social factor. (Barnett 1933, 1)

These words of Professor George E. Barnett of Johns Hopkins University in his American Economic Association presidential address of December 1932 preceded Franklin D. Roosevelt's and John L. Lewis's remaking of American industrialism.

The American environment has imprinted certain features on collective bargaining which we identify as (1) adversarialism, (2) economism, (3) protectivism, (4) rationalization, (5) the tradeoff, (6) gamesmanship, and (7) power.

According to the adversarial mode in industrial relations, the union's "main job is to challenge and protest managerial actions" (Harbison and Coleman 1951, 20); management's main job is to resist. The American parties stop short of pursuing adversarialism to the point of a transcending class struggle by periodically agreeing to the main terms of the relationship. In this and other respects, the adversarial relationship has been normalized through due process methods like grievance-arbitration. From time to time unions and managements in various industries have even aspired to more constructive, integrative, problem-solving, and trusting relationships, but such relationships have been forced eventually to revert to the adversarial type.

Management persists in the adversary relationship because it fears that, otherwise, union collaboration would dilute management power and thereby impair efficiency. The union continues to prefer the adversary relationship because it is most compatible with the union's bargaining effectiveness. The less the union takes responsibility for making joint decisions with management the more credibly it feels it can "grieve" over the decisions later. The adversary principle, it is argued in a variation on Adam Smith's invisible hand, also best serves the public or general interest. The assumption is that the parties can be kept "honest," so to speak, only by the countervailing checks and balances which the adversarial tension produces. ("Tension" is probably a better word than "conflict" to describe the nature of the employer-employee interaction. Conflict implies one side winning over the other; tension implies equilibrium or a balance of forces—which is what collective bagaining and industrial relations are more nearly about.)

Once again, some theoreticians and practitioners are questioning whether adversarialism is really the best of all possible worlds. This time it is the economic reversal that is prompting a reevaluation of this position. There is additionaly the possibility that some part of the Japanese "miracle" can be attributed to the collaborative spirit in Japanese industrial relations. Experiments in quality of worklife and codetermination are testing out the proposition that the adversary relationship at the bargaining table can coexist fruitfully with a collaborative attitude on the shop or office floor or in the boardroom. The evidence is not in yet. The only thing that can be said now is that a few unions and managements are willing to risk serious experiments.

These undertakings are forcing the workers, particularly, to face up to the duality of their interests. On the one hand, the union's objective is to get as much as it can for its constituents; on the other, the ability of the union to get what it wants depends squarely on the ability of the enterprise to perform efficiently. Workers and unions knew this intuitively, of course, but the symbol of the union as a fighting adversary organization has always overshadowed the common interests of the parties. And it is also the fighting face of the union that has, up to now, dominated its rhetoric and personality.

Economism is the tendency of collective bargaining to deal only with terms that translate easily into some sort of price—that is, into wages, hours, and so on. In recent years collective bargaining's coolness to negotiation of the quality of work has been cited as an example of economism and the excessive preoccupation with "more."

Closely related to adversarialism is protectivism, the attitude that the bargainers dare not let their guards down lest they be taken in by the other side. The ruling maxim in the protective outlook is, Play it close to the chest. The bargainers develop a hypersensitivity to anything that threatens to impair the power equilibrium. The disposition to nail everything down leaves very little to trust and goodwill. This is why, contrary to the hopes of the early collective bargaining philosophers, contracts have become longer and processes, including arbitration, have become more formalized—more "legalistic" is the way it is usually put.

Rationalization means the tendency of bargaining to take on highly structured and institutionalized forms. From an evolutionary standpoint, rationalization represented an advance over earlier catch-as-catch-can and thrust-and-parry. But now three- and four-step grievance-arbitration systems, 100-plus-page written agreements, the rituals of bargaining and negotiation, the intricacies of internal union processes, and politics have all introduced bureaucratic elements into the relationship. While these structures are undoubtedly an improvement over the trial by ordeal of the past, they nevertheless generate problems of their own, including rank-and-file disaffection and apathy. Rationalization is of a piece with the power equilibrium in that it springs from the need to constrain the exercise of discretion by resorting to a body of rules and procedures.

The tradeoff syndrome demands some kind of symbolic symmetry in the concessions which each side makes. Union bargainers have to be in a position to demonstrate that union "give-ups" are matched by management "give-ups." In this time of wage concession much ill-feeling has been caused by the refusal of some managements to make the sorts of concessions which they have been urging on their employees.

The gamesmanship of negotiations is the "immense amount of palaver, playacting, game playing and general emotional hullaba-loo" (Boulding 1953, 101) as the union acts to maintain its cred-ibility on two fronts: the negotiating table and its rank-and-file constituency.

The counters in the collective bargaining game are still price and power. The game is still about the union and its constituents, who seek to enhance the price of labor and their power positions. Man-agement's role is to try to contain the union price and power drive.

It is not only that collective bargaining brings higher costs which evoke management resistance, but that negotiation necessarily brings with it an erosion of management authority over how labor is to be utilized. This is why the stakes in collective bargaining are both price and power. The price-power symbiosis has been ob-scured because price is measurable while power is not.

So, much about collective bargaining remains unchanged; nor is there any prospect that it will change in the foreseeable future even though the philosophers and prophets of collective bargain-ing—terms that are not meant unkindly—have always looked for-ward to the day when a more constructive relationship could re-place the pulling and hauling of the price-power distributive game.

If the basic character of the game has not changed, the way the game is played has surely changed. The word that comes closest to conveying the essence of the change is "civilized." Other words conveying the same connotation are "rationalized," "normal-ized," "routinized." One dictionary defines "civilize" as "to bring out of a savage state." It is not too extreme to think about collective bargaining as having brought the employer-employee relationship "out of a savage state" compared to the arbitrariness, turbulence, class warfare, and violence that marked it in the past, and once in a while still does.

Collective bargaining has civilized the determination of the price of labor by negotiating a wage structure, and not only an hourly wage. "Civilize," or perhaps "humanize," is not inappro-priate to describe what has happened to the compensation system, which allocates an increasingly larger share toward human maintenance—i.e., health, retirement, leisure—over the employee's career. "Civilize," in the sense of "normalize," describes modifications by formulas instead of by haggling, as in adjusting to changes in the cost of living and productivity.

The power relationships between the parties have also been normalized. Most strikes and other sanctions are no longer perceived as rebellions or ends in themselves but simply as the withholding capability essential to bargaining of any sort. The uses of power in bargaining are normalized through complex organizations which the parties establish to deal with each other and to administer their internal affairs—organizations which are frequently manned by technical and professional staff. The parties' election to maintain collective bargaining as a price-power distributive game has not been due to the lack of experimentation with problem-solving alternatives, but very little of the experimentation has stuck.

Collective bargaining seems mostly suited to incremental change. The short-term horizon of workers makes it difficult for them to adjust easily to wholesale change. Employers, for their part, while better adjusted to longer time-horizons in their business affairs, resist wholesale change in their labor dealings. Employers oppose all bargaining innovations at first and will, under pressure, accept them only if they are undertaken piecemeal. Eventually employers come to see positive merit in an innovation, but this evolves from experience and not from rational precalculation.

Collective bargaining has undoubtedly lessened the tensions incident to employment. It has eased the harshness of the hierarchical organization in industry by introducing rights, orderly procedures, and a measure of self-determination at work. It has made feasible higher standards of consumption for working people. Collective bargaining's shock effect has stirred management, whether unionized or not, to adopt a more humane conception of its role and a more efficient direction of its labor force.

# CHAPTER EIGHT

# The State in Industrial Relations

THE PLURALISTIC STATE has functioned at various times as an ally of business, workers, and unions. In modern times the state has consciously struck out on its own. It has tried to rise above partisan interests to serve what it deems to be a public or general interest.

Up to the 1930s, custom, tradition, and class power, more than law, set the rules of industrial relations in the United States. From the 1930s on, the rules have been codified into statutes, administrative regulations, and court decisions at both the state and local levels. The consensus view has been that the law "is relatively more procedural, leaving the substantive conditions of employment and the rules of work place—wages, benefits, hours and working conditions—to negotiating parties" (Dunlop 1973, 48). It will be argued here, among other things, that the rules established by law not only formulate the procedures for bargaining but, in the process, are also likely to shape the direction of the results.

The state regulates seven areas bearing on collective bargaining and industrial relations: (1) private and public sector labor relations, (2) labor standards, (3) social welfare, (4) the labor market, (5) wage-price stability, (6) equal opportunity, and (7) information.

The government's rules for labor relations in the private sector aim to protect unions, managements, and union members from one another's "unfair" practices. The rules also regulate the uses of union sanctions like picketing, secondary boycotts, and jurisdictional strikes, and management counter-sanctions like injunctions. Finally, rules of law establish procedures for representation disputes, the conduct of union government, and the resolution of conflict, including mediation, arbitration, and fact-finding. The state sets guidelines for public sector bargaining, emphasizing particularly methods of dispute resolution other than the strike.

The law of labor standards deals with the compensation, hours, and working conditions of private sector employees. Davis-Bacon, Walsh-Healy, and the Fair Labor Standards Act are the historic federal examples here. The first two regulate labor standards in construction and manufacturing under federal contract. The last sets standards for employment which affects interstate commerce in general. More recently the federal regulation of compensation has been enlarged to include private pension plans. Standards relating to physical working conditions range from the long-established factory laws in the states to the comprehensive and still-to-be-digested occupational health and safety legislation (OSHA) passed in 1970.

Social welfare regulation covers social insurance and social security, including income supports for the aged, unemployed, indigent, and occupationally impaired. Labor market policy deals with full (high-level) employment and the improvement of those labor market institutions—training, education, employment services, guidance, and planning—necessary to make full employment operative. Income or wage policy (which has been stop-and-go more than continuous) undertakes to "stabilize" wages and prices to cope with the threat of the inflation which is associated with full employment.

Equal opportunity regulation attempts to eliminate race, sex, and age barriers to full participation in the labor market. The information function is represented in the design, collection, and dissemination of statistics which register the state of the economy and society. Running through all of these areas of intervention is the management of monetary and fiscal policy to back up the not always compatible objectives of high-level employment, anti-inflation, and a favorable business climate, the degree of emphasis on one or another varying with the ideology of the administration in power.

The federal government has largely taken over the regulation of industrial relations. Within the federal structure the courts have been responsible for the most sweeping reforms, particularly in the realm of antidiscrimination in employment. The quality of the

American intervention in industrial relations is conveyed by the common use of the word "intervention" to describe the process. "Intervention" suggests, in the first place perhaps, the "unnaturalness" of the state's role in economic affairs in the United States, by contrast with the more "natural" role of regulation in most other industrial societies. The American mode of intervention is ad hoc, piecemeal, incremental, and opportunistic. It is more responsive to exigencies of the moment than to policy frameworks.

I concentrate here on three major tendencies in the development of the American regulatory scheme in industrial relations: (1) positive public policy, (2) substantive regulation, and (3) the Reagan turnaround.

President Kennedy defined the spirit of *positive* public policy as "sophisticated solutions to complex and obstinate issues, . . . not some grand warfare of rival ideologies which will sweep the country with passion but the practical management of a modern economy" (Kennedy 1962, 20). Positive public policy purports to be above class. It reflects the apprehension that bilateral bargaining does not sufficiently take into account the macro effects of bargaining results. Therefore, as the Kennedy Secretary of Labor Arthur J. Goldberg said, government has to "assert and define the national interest" (Goldberg 1966, 142).

Positive public policy contrasts with partisan public policy. On the eve of the New Deal a pro-employer policy prevailed. As a contemporary account put it: "Employers, for all practical purposes, enjoy complete freedom of combination in their dealings with employees. . . . They can deal with unions or not as they see fit. In times of trouble they have a free hand to employ strikebreakers or refuse to employ workmen because of union membership and, to all practical intents and purposes, can with immunity resort to the blacklist if they so choose" (Witte 1932, 80).

There were some countertrends during this time. The Clayton Act (1914) declared "that the labor of a human being is not a commodity or article of commerce." It was initially hailed by the labor movement as the "magna carta" which would liberate it from the evil of the federal labor injunction. In fact, this did not happen until after the passage of the Norris-LaGuardia Act in 1932. President Wilson's policy for disputes settlement during World War I served the unions so well that the level of union membership achieved in the war years would not be surpassed until after the New Deal. The Railway Labor Act (1926), a forerunner of the Wagner Act, established procedures for disputes settlement and protected railroad workers' rights to collective bargaining.

The Norris-LaGuardia Act (1932) "ushered in a period of almost complete freedom for union expansion" (Gregory 1961, 223). Norris-LaGuardia denied federal courts the right to issue injunctions in labor disputes. Section 7a of the National Industrial Recovery Act followed a year later. Section 7a—the price demanded by the unions for their support of the National Industrial Recovery Act as a whole—outlawed company unions and gave employees the right to unions of their own choosing.

The high point of pro-union public policy came with the passage of the Wagner Act (National Labor Relations Act) in 1935 and its validation by a narrow majority of the Supreme Court two years later. The act set off the collective bargaining revolution in mass production industry. It outlawed unfair employer practices and gave workers the right to elect an exclusive bargaining representative with whom the employer was legally obligated to negotiate if requested.

The Taft-Hartley Act (the Labor-Management Relations Act, 1947), passed by the first Republican Congress since 1930, marked an ebbing of union influence. Taft-Hartley took over much of the unfair employer practices of Wagner but, in addition, protected employers against *union* unfair labor practices, implementing the new legislative finding "that certain practices by some labor organizations, their officers, and members" can also "impair the interest of the public."

The Labor-Management Reporting and Disclosure Act of 1959 (Landrum-Griffin) represented mixed intentions. On the one hand it strengthened employers' protection against the secondary boycott. But, on the other, it took off on a new theme in labor relations policy: union members were to be protected not only against employers but also against union officers. For the most part the AFL-CIO supported this doctrine, as did many pro-union members of Congress. Employers supported it too, but they were probably less interested in union democracy than they were in checking the power of union leaders. Landrum-Griffin represented the beginnings of what I am calling positive public policy because government seemed here to be intervening in industrial relations on more independent terms, or at least on terms which went beyond—even if haltingly—the claims of the parties at interest.

Enactments from the 1960s on in civil rights, labor market and incomes policies, occupational health and safety, and pension reform represented even stronger assertions of positive public policy. Labor as resource rather than labor in unions and collective bargaining became the focus of public policy in this period. In some respects civil rights and incomes policies have an almost anti-union character.

Labor market policy began by dealing with immediate needs as they arose: the "competitively disadvantaged—unemployed, underemployed, low-income earners, youth, older workers, nonwhites, those with low education levels, etc." (U.S. Cabinet Committee on Price Stability 1969, 26). Later, labor market policy began to look toward an American version of the Swedish "active manpower policy" wherein labor market policy becomes "a promising complement to the traditional [fiscal and monetary] tools of economic policy" (USDL 1970, 7–8).

Wage-price policy has been "neutral" or positive in the somewhat perverse sense that it was unacceptable both to unions and business and to most government policymakers. Only economists have supported it, and they are far from unanimous in this support. The policy for equal opportunity is also neutral as against both management and unions. In its reactive stage civil rights policy moved to prohibit discrimination in employment. But a reactive policy of no-discrimination had to be reenforced by the more positive "affirmative action." Affirmative action operates on the principle that equal opportunity cannot be achieved passively, simply by sending up the normal labor market signals and waiting for disadvantaged workers to respond. The theory of affirmative action also demanded employer and union initiatives in hiring and upgrading minorities and women, initiatives which are normally not forthcoming except under government pressure.

Positive public policy seems to have evolved in two stages. In the reactive stage, public policy intervention, although neutral, is nevertheless bound by the terms of reference set by the union-management parties. In the initiative stage intervention moves on-to a new plane based less on the positions of the parties and more on presumptively objective or scientific grounds advanced by the government spokesmen or by other "third" parties.

Positive public policy in one field coexists with pressure group policy in others. Republican appointees to the National Labor Relations Board are more likely to be employer-leaning than are Democratic appointments, and vice versa. A Republican president is unlikely to say, as President Johnson did: "I have met with Mr. Meany and his assistants many times but with Mr. Meany 49 times, in personal meetings either in my office, the Oval Room or in the mansion. In addition . . . he has called me, or I have called him 82 additional times" (Johnson 1969, 7). Teamster support of President Nixon and President Reagan seems to have paid off in gaining for that union a special relationship with the administration.

The regulation of bargaining procedures has led the law ineluctably into shaping substantive outcomes. Nowhere is this more apparent than in the National Labor Relations Act. The NLRB's authority to determine the appropriate bargaining unit, although based on objective criteria, may nonetheless "assist one of the parties in the competition for or against representation" (Samoff 1970, 704). No one can know for sure how much, but the NLRB's early support of inclusive units undoubtedly advanced the fortunes of the industrial unions in their challenge to the craft union hegemony. In the view of a prominent craft union spokesman, government exerted a major influence on the "form and character of organization that shall hereafter prevail in the labor movement" (Woll 1960, 419). Working in the other direction, the Railway Labor Act acted to preserve the craft structure of the established railroad unions for a long time after objective circumstances had rendered craft unionism obsolete (U.S. National Mediation Board 1950, 17).

The history of bargaining over health and pension plans, subcontracting, relocation, and plant closings demonstrates that the obligation to bargain in good faith over these subjects, even if not requiring agreement, nonetheless created an irresistible magnetic field for the consummation of agreements (Wellington 1968, 73 ff.). Similarly, NLRB decisions to take jurisdiction over a firm or industry have invariably ended with agreements in classes of enterprises which, but for this circumstance, would have been able to resist bargaining. From a static viewpoint the NLRB's jurisdiction is procedural. In a dynamic context the board's decision to take jurisdiction sets up a chain of circumstances which almost inevitably culminates in agreement, even if not necessarily required by law. Modern examples of this symbiosis include proprietary hospitals, nursing homes, private college faculties, and professional athletics.

There are categories of law which, if they do not determine, nonetheless materially affect, the bargaining result. The legal constraints stop something short of forcing a specific outcome but strongly predispose the bargaining result toward a settlement materially different from what it might otherwise be.

Laws which regulate wages—like the Fair Labor Standards Act, Walsh-Healy, and Davis-Bacon—put a wage floor under nonunion competition and have had the effect of raising the threshold from which the wage bargaining starts. Another type of intervention shifts the financing of previously negotiated programs from the collective bargaining fund to public sources. The effect is frequently to stretch the buying power of the collective bargaining fund to include new benefits. Medicare relieved the collective bargaining "kitty" of the retiree's health insurance benefits and put the union in a favorable tactical position to demand newer benefits.

Law constrains substantive outcomes by raising union consciousness of a problem. The best and current case is the pump-priming effect of the Occupational Safety and Health Act (OSHA) on union demands in occupational health and safety. Subsidy laws, as in the maritime industry, support maritime union wage goals because they enable U.S. flag operators "to offset the difference between the high costs [mostly wage costs] and the lower costs of their foreign competitors" (Jautscher 1973, 763).

State intervention, according to modern voluntarism, should be limited to the referee's role—that is, to the function of setting and monitoring rules, but not determining results. The rules should be focused on the maintenance of a power balance among the parties.

It is too early to tell whether the Reagan labor policy simply continues the trend of union restraint begun with Taft-Hartley and extended with Landrum-Griffin, or, alternatively, whether it represents a wholesale reversion to the pro-business labor climate of the Coolidge-Hoover 1920s. The labor policy of the Nixon-Ford administrations, by way of comparison between Republican administrations, was not noticeably different from that of their Democratic predecessors.

The Reagan administration has moved the trade unions out from their insiders' position for the first time in half a century. Unions have suffered political defeats in the past, but never before have they felt as totally excluded from the centers of government power as they are now. Even the Department of Labor, the traditional union conduit to the executive branch, is now out of reach.

Supply-side economics, or Reaganomics, translates into an implicit—at times explicit—incomes policy which has had as its object the curtailment of union power and wage repression. The unions have not been asked to cooperate in this policy, as they were in the more explicit incomes policies of the past, nor, for that matter, would they. The Reagan incomes policy has not been a case, as Murray Weidenbaum, Council of Economic Advisors chairman, said, of "telling labor and management what to do." Rather, it has been a strategy of "subjecting them to the fundamental forces of the market" (Weidenbaum 1981, B2). The fundamental force of the market shaping this incomes policy has been the highest unemployment since the Great Depression. Combined with another fundamental force of the market—high interest rates—the deflation or disinflation effect has fashioned an environment decidedly unfavorable to union advances.

Reaganomics is not all that special in singling out oversized collective bargaining settlements as the hard core of inflation. This doctrine has long been a staple of mainline economics and, whenever politically feasible, of public wage policy.

Reagan labor policy is bringing about sweeping changes in labor law administration and policy. While pro-labor statutes have no-where been repealed outright, an equivalent effect, without the po-litical turmoil, is being accomplished through administrative regulation and the appointment process. Bacon-Davis, minimum wage, and occupational health and safety are undergoing amend-ment by rule and by administrative emphasis and deemphasis; the Department of Labor, the National Labor Relations Board, the Equal Employment Opportunities Commission, and the Occupa-tional Safety and Health Administration are increasingly being ad-ministered by Reagan appointees who have made no secret of their reservations about the laws which they are administering.

This political "take-away and give-back" strategy is not at all inconsistent with Reagan doctrine, which, from the union view-point, is fostering not only a tax-free, but also a regulation-free and, as part of that, a union-free environment to encourage busi-ness to invest. (A recent example of the last—unsuccessful as it happened—was permitting nursing homes to deduct union-busting expense as legitimate costs.) Reagan spokesmen disclaim antilabor intentions. Eventually, they argue, these policies will re-dound to the union advantage by encouraging a favorable in-vestment climate and, as a consequence, a favorable employment condition.

The air controllers' strike of 1981 provides a scenario of what a *New York Times* commentary called "the execution of a union" (S. Taylor 1981, A14): gross mismanagement of personnel by the FAA, impossibilist demands and gross miscalculations by the union, and government retaliation by mass dismissals, contempt citations, and decertification—all of which put an end to the strike and to the union.

There could be in the making a major redirection of state power against union interests as radical as the revolution in the other di-rection wrought by Roosevelt's New Deal. In any case, the era of positive public policy has come to a halt, and in process is a pro-employer policy.

More than a half-century ago John R. Commons, America's preeminent scholar of industrial relations, called for a "new equity that will protect the job as the older equity protected the business"

(Commons 1924, 307). American labor law made great strides toward the achievement of that new equity. This is how workers' rights stood on the eve of the Reagan presidency: Short of an outright entitlement to a job there appeared to be a national consensus that high-level employment with "tolerable" levels of unemployment represented the highest priority of public policy. Victims of unemployment and other economic insecurities were entitled to varying forms of income protection. Large numbers of employees had legally enforceable rights to a "minimum" or "prevailing" wage, to a safe workplace, to protection against discrimination because of race, sex, age, and union membership, to concerted economic activity in a union, and to adequate education and training.

The worker as a union member had a right to financial information relating to his union, to speak up in the union, to be fairly represented, and to engage in union activity free from coercion by management or by union officials. The union was entitled to organize, to strike and picket peacefully for most purposes, and to bargain with an appropriate employer. The employer was entitled to protection from specified coercive acts of the union.

It is possible that Reagan labor policy represents the strongest reaction yet against the new equity, although a reaction has been in the making for a long time. Some of the questions raised by these reactions are, Is the work ethic being eroded by the welfare state? Is near-full employment a bearable burden in terms of its inflation costs? Do the unions, therefore, have too much power in an age of inflation? Are the claims of the new equity beyond our present resources? Has the new equity brought with it a new bureaucracy? And finally, has "the growth of regulations and law . . . far outstripped our capacity to develop consensus and mutual accommodations to our common detriment" (Dunlop 1976, 74)?

## CHAPTER NINE

# Comparative Industrial Relations

THIS CHAPTER undertakes to provide a basis for examining American industrial relations in a larger frame by comparison with other countries. The intent is comparisons by broad categories rather than country by country. The structure of industrial relations laid out here is a product of Western advanced capitalisms and the social democracy of North America and Western Europe; or, in capsule terms, of the private ownership and management of the means of production as modified by a welfare state. The essential attribute of Western industrial relations is the considerable independence of the employers and management on one side and unions and workers on the other in bargaining out the terms of their relationship relatively free from surveillance by the state.

"Relatively" is meant to suggest that no institution in modern societies can function entirely free of state influence. But there is a difference, to put it in polar terms, between the kinds of constraints imposed on industrial relations by Western political systems and the integration of industrial relations into the state system characteristic of the Soviet-type systems and of many of the developing societies. The difference is basically between pluralistic and unitary industrial relations.

There are, further, important differences *within* the Western pluralistic model. The variations range from the relatively loose ties between industrial relations and state power and public policy in the United States and Canada, on the one hand, and the regulatory frameworks of, say, France, West Germany, Sweden, and Austria, on the other. Nonetheless, the industrial relations parties both in North America and Western Europe (or the social partners, as the West Europeans say) are each capable of pursuing independent courses of policy and action, as they have demonstrated many times. They are also capable of agreeing with their respective governments on common courses of action. Consensus is achieved by a "social contract" among approximate equals, not by edict. Poland is only the latest example of what happens to a union movement in the Soviet-type system which aspires to independence.

The differences between pluralistic and unitary industrial relations represent, at bottom, differences in history and social development. Bargaining in industrial relations is more compatible with a market system than with socialist central planning. The more the state intervenes in market systems the greater are the difficulties which the bargaining process encounters. Unemployment, inflation, and payments imbalances have forced liberal states to intervene more and more in the market and have, to this degree, disturbed the two-party equilibrium of industrial relations.

The bargaining approach to decisionmaking in industrial relations has been able to function in the West because the parties, to begin with, have achieved an equilibrium of power for more than a generation. Only when the employer-union bargain evolved from a social struggle into a transaction did the parties begin to routinize their relationship. It is at this point that the process of professionalization begins. For the union professionalization means that union representation develops into a full-time vocation and the union becomes a complex organization. Simultaneously, bargaining success begins to sap the revolutionary commitment, even if the union rhetoric does not always show it.

Mass education imbues the working classes with the self-confidence necessary for effectiveness in bargaining. The ability to read, write, and count makes it possible for the workers to develop their own leaders, draft their own constitutions, keep their own books of account, write their own contracts, and write up their own grievances without having to bring in middle-class technicians. After a while, union administration becomes a profession in its own right.

For the managements in the advanced capitalisms professionalization has been part of the general rationalization process which is the essence of modern management. Management's in-

creasing skill in the bargaining game made possible by rationalization is an important element in its willingness to come to terms
with collective bargaining.

It is the nature of bargaining that, more than any other mode of
joint dealing, it places the parties in a posture of relative equality,
whatever their relative social status is otherwise. The industrial
relations backwardness of the retarded capitalisms—Spain, Por-
tugal, Russia—began precisely with their ingrained incapacity to
deal with their workers as equals.

The purpose of the bargaining game is the achievement of mutually satisfying terms of exchange. Although there is a measure of
satisfaction in playing the game for its own sake, eventually the
parties have to achieve some sort of acceptable payout or the bargaining process atrophies. In North America the scarcity of labor
provided economic leverage for wage payout and thereby made
recourse to political and revolutionary methods less urgent.
Similarly, bargaining falls something short of yielding up an acceptable return in an economy of labor surpluses. To that degree
politics and revolution become more attractive to workers.

There is no need to own the means of production if it is possible
to bargain effectively with those who do, as Selig Perlman instructed us a long time ago. And when workers could not gain all
they wanted on their own, they turned to "the method of legal
enactment" in a democratic pluralistic state. The socialist option
was further discouraged in the United States by the relatively early
achievement of the popular franchise and mass education, which
deprived the revolutionary impulse of a significant wellspring of
working-class injustice.

The ability of social democracies to cope, even if imperfectly,
with the evils of poverty, mass unemployment, impoverished old
age, low wages, and ill health went far to undercut the Marxist
prophecy of mass immiseration and capitalist collapse. Marx, bas-
ing his system on what he had observed in Europe's 1840s and
'50s, had understandably discounted Western capitalism's subsequent ability to change and resort to "if you can't beat 'em, join
'em." Liberal, bargaining-type industrial relations withered on
the vine precisely where the working class was incapable of mount-
ing an effective social democratic challenge to an unregenerate

capitalism and where the capitalists and the state power either refused to listen or were incapable of it.

But it is wise to stress that we are still talking in relative and "more or less" terms. France and Italy, although in the Western capitalist mold because their industrial relations institutions wield considerable independent power, depart from the ideal type at several points. Italy, particularly, suffers from enclaves of underdevelopment and labor surpluses. Multiunionism and the methods of direct action and mass demonstration still figure prominently in the French-Italian model, as do influential communist and neo-Christian movements, militant employers, a relatively underdeveloped management, and a pervasive state, none of which are present in the same degree in the other Western societies.

The central and northern European movements—notably those in West Germany, the Scandinavian countries and the Netherlands—represent still another variation on the pluralistic industrial relations model. Central European employers have been more accepting of unions as the spokesmen of the working class. There is nothing like the challenge to the existence of the union as an institution that still prevails in the United States. Nor is there in North America anything like the politics of labor parties, socialism and social democracy, the debates over nationalization of industry, and codetermination that figure so vitally in the industrial relations of central and Scandinavian Europe. The North American difference is largely due to the failure of a socialist ideology to take hold among the masses.

In Western Europe the idea of a labor movement encompasses not only the union but also the political party and, to a somewhat lesser degree in recent times, the cooperatives. Bargaining in Western Europe is also more centralized. Nonetheless, Western Europe's industrial relations at the bargaining table and on the shop floor share with North America a considerable independence from the state authority.

European industrial relations is now being rocked by the same forces which are reshaping industrial relations in the United States—but in Europe, unlike North America, the effect has been to reinvigorate radicalism, not so much communist as anti-capitalist radicalism. The end of economic growth has combined with European labor's left turn to weaken, if not destroy, the *entente cordiale* between unions and employers that had marked the industrial relations of central and Scandinavian Europe.

In a category all of its own is Japan. Japan partakes of enough of the attributes of the advanced industrial society to put it in the Western camp of advanced capitalism. At the same time, Japan deviates—or is said to deviate (there are many dissenters)—sharply from the Western model at critical points. Whereas the main-line Western model is essentially a conflict model with just enough collaboration and consensus to get goods and services produced more or less competitively, the Japanese model is arguably just the reverse: a basic consensus modified at the margin by conflict.

The Japanese variant—or, if, one is critical of it, the Japanese "stereotype"—carries with it such attitudes as "paternalism, loyalty, commitment, harmony, consensus" (Shimada 1980, 7) or, as Japanese scholarship has analyzed it, a species of "groupism." Groupism "is a way of thinking in which people put preference for group interests before individual ones in relations between group and individual" (Ishikawa 1982, 10). The consensual model is reenforced by such well-known features as the seniority system and lifetime employment. In our terms of reference what Japanese management has done essentially is to buy out the work society's resistance to increased efficiency by security guarantees, which is a viable option in a high-growth economy.

Collective bargaining as the centerpiece of Western industrial relations had its origins and development, to sum it up, in the symbiosis of Western capitalism and social democracy and their attendant economic, social, and political circumstances. As the salient features in the Western collective bargaining context we can single out labor scarcity, the market system, gradual economic growth, an "affluent society," pluralistic democracy, a mediating middle class, mass education, and the legitimacy of the strike.

Industrial relations in the developing societies—functioning in the context of intense nationalist feeling, anticolonialism, new nationhood, labor surpluses, rising expectations, illiteracy, polarized social structures, systematic planning, one-commodity economies and one-party states, and the absence of a mediating middle class—are necessarily producing industrial relations institutions that differ sharply from those of the West. In general, instead of more or less autonomy, industrial relations in the developing society becomes highly dependent on and almost completely attuned to the state's purposes.

The private sector workplace in the developing societies is more likely to be directed by an owner-employer than by a professional manager. "Attention [is] to rules rather than to output and profit, to status and seniority rather than to efficiency and initiative." Management is more often "dynastic than dynamic"; that is, "the enterprise begins to stagnate in its family traditions" and resists the "infusion of talent from outside the closed circle of group or family" (Khatkhate 1971, 10, 12).

This lower order of labor cost discipline has its origins in labor-surplus economies, where a plentiful labor supply makes rationalized management less necessary. By contrast, it has been labor scarcity that spurred the employing classes in the developed economies of Western Europe and North America toward professionalization and the economical uses of labor.

Rural labor's weak commitment to wage employment in the developing economies has made it difficult to build a protective work society which could effectively counter employer exploitation on its own: "The worker is so little connected with industrial life and so bereft of power and the basis for organizing power that he has neither a great desire nor sufficient means to protest" (Kerr 1964, 335). On the shop floor the new worker lacks the discipline which is the first condition for an industrialized labor force:

> Earlier as an agricultural worker he has not had to abide by specific hours of work, prescribed speed. He was practically free to determine the method and pace of work. His relations with his landlord were cordial and often he was treated as a minor member of the family. When he becomes an industrial worker, he is expected to go to the factory at a particular time, work therein for a specified time with a minimum prescribed

speed, abide by the various rules and regulations regarding work and safety, and strictly follow the factory discipline. (Mehta 1957, 23)

Yet, despite differences in commitment, work societies in the developing economies react very much like workers in the more industrialized societies. Indiscipline in the work society is universal, including turnover, absenteeism, and even ''more violent expression in fighting, spontaneous flare-ups and work stoppage by small groups and even machine or parts breakage and sabotage to the production process'' (Kerr 1964, 173–74). Low commitment combined with a labor surplus tends to negate the union's regulation of its labor supply, which is a condition for regulating labor's price. This is why the unions must rely mostly on the state to enforce a closed shop and minimum wage.

Exploitation alone is hardly ever a sufficient condition for workers to band together in an economic association. Also required is social cohesiveness. In the formative period in the United States craft consciousness served such a purpose, as did the civil rights movement for black workers and the Chicano farm workers later. The unions in the developing societies owe much of their momentum and solidarity to the struggle for nationhood and independence.

The same nationalism that serves to bind workers together in a union also acts as a force of repression on the union when the nationalists achieve power. The unions in developing societies are continuously under pressure to subordinate their workplace interests to the ''national interest'' in economic growth and national awareness. The result has been a unionism which partakes more of the mass movement and sometimes of an angry crowd than of a structured bargaining organization.

The unions in the developing societies are made up of workers who are recent migrants from the countryside, poorly paid, and, in the words of an Indian trade union pioneer, ''illiterate, ignorant and backward'' (Karnik 1969, 292). When they associate themselves in a union their status is more like followers than members. ''The main defect of Asian trade unions,'' Asoka Mehta has said, ''are their unsound finances, low and irregular membership, faulty administration and accounts with lack of experience and maturity among union leaders, exploitation for political purposes, rivalry and multiplicity of unions, loose structure at various levels, and heavy reliance on government machinery'' (Mehta 1957, 16).

The fledgling unions in the West could rely on a cadre of crafts-men to provide leadership. Lacking this craft cadre (Kassalow 1969, 293), the unions in developing societies have had to turn to political, middle-class leaders to represent them in their dealings with employers and government. But this also has contributed to the use of the union ''as a power base for politicians [including] identification, very close cooperation . . . or even integration of trade unions and political parties; occupation of government func-tions and trade union posts at the same time; . . . and changes in the industrial relations system to accommodate it to the ideology of the group in power'' (Essenberg 1981, 91).

The union organization in developing societies frequently has to go beyond bargaining in serving membership interests and needs because the conventional subject matter of bargaining has, in ef-fect, been preempted as a government function. Consumer coop-eratives are one of these essential services. The trade unions of Singapore, for example, finding their bargaining function limited by law, turned to insurance, taxi services, and dental care. Kenya unions sponsor banks and cooperatives, and in Ghana the unions have organized a labor education college, housing, and health and credit union services (Gladstone 1979, 9; see also Paladino 1979, 24 ff.).

The strike in the developing industrial relations systems is fre-quently an act of protest with demands not always related to the employer's competence. The agreement ending the strike is likely to be a brief memorandum. It is like a temporary armistice or cease-fire in a permanent campaign of guerilla warfare in which neither side concedes the legitimacy of the other's function or exis-tence.

The unions in the new nations are either instruments of the rul-ing political authority, in which case the union is managed so as not to threaten the ruling power or their goals for economic devel-opment; or the unions become instruments of an organized op-position committed to overturning the ruling authority, in which case the unions are either outlawed, obstructed, or suppressed. The idea of autonomous unions, free to support or oppose the government as a "loyal opposition," is foreign to industrial relations experience and theories in developing societies.

The way the union in developing economics is organized flows from these political uses of the union. The union is structured only enough for the leadership to bring the masses out in the streets. Constitutions, conventions, regular meetings, strike votes, checks and balances, dispersion of power through committees, and all the other hallmarks of structured government or organizations are, for the most part, absent. This is not too different from the beginnings of unionism in the West. Allowing for important cultural differences, there has been a considerable element of ideology, millennialism, cultism, and ritual in every beginning workers' movement.

The state maintains its tutelage over the unions and collective bargaining because the political leadership is not prepared to tolerate independent centers of political and economic power; and if the political leaders are not themselves communists, they are not prepared to tolerate communist control of the union. For example,

> Indian trade unions, though weak in comparison to their counterparts in the developed countries of the West, have been great foci of potential political power. Their power is bound to grow with industrialization, legal protection and political encouragement. It is, therefore, no wonder that the leadership of the Indian National Congress could clearly see that whoever wielded this power would ultimately control the stability and progress of the industrialized sector and through it, eventually the destiny of the country. The labour wing of the Indian National Congress supported by some of its powerful leaders could not take the risk of letting this power slip into the hands of the communists. It was therefore decided at the party level to intervene decisively in the trade union movement and acquire political control over a large section of it. (Johri 1967, 9–10)

State control of union-employer relationships in developing societies, particularly in Latin America, has been described as corporatism, after the corporations established under Italian fascism. It has been defined as:

(1) state structuring of groups that produces a system of officially sanctioned, noncompetitive, compulsory interest associations,

(2) state *subsidy* of these groups and

(3) state imposed *constraints* on demand-making, leadership and internal governance.

Corporatism is thus a non-pluralist system of group representation. (Collier and Collier 1979, 968)

Corporatism is differentiated from the general run of intervention by the highly structured character of the controls, which include registration, monopoly of representation, compulsory membership, and union subsidies. The corporatist system exercises control over strikes and leadership, and monitors and intervenes systematically in union affairs (ibid., 971).

Another variation on industrial relations in a developing society is represented by South Korea. South Korea departs somewhat from type in maintaining a strong private sector, albeit under a government with a "single-minded commitment to economic growth and . . . export-led development" (Westphal 1982, 38). As an essential element in that rapid growth, unions are permitted, "but genuine collective bargaining is prohibited" (Bognanno and Kim 1981, 201). Perhaps Taiwan, China, and Singapore represent the same combination of authoritarian government, a vigorous private sector, and unionism and collective bargaining under restraint.

Industrial relations in the centrally planned socialist systems differs fundamentally from the Western systems, although terms like "collective agreements," "trade unions," "strikes," and so on, are common to both. Socialist industrial relations has this much in common with the developing societies: both attempt to use industrial relations as a system of labor control to assure conformity with

*125*

the interests and goals of the state. The difference is in the efficacy of the respective control systems. In Soviet-type systems, controls are highly formalized, institutionalized, structured, and very effective in maintaining state hegemony, although protests and even rebellions are not unusual. But in the developing societies totalistic institutions come into conflict with deep-rooted decentralizing influences in the culture. Even when ruling groups are not averse to exerting total power they simply lack the technique, temperament, and institutions for the task.

The essential difference between socialist and Western industrial relations is that in the former workers do not have the bargaining power that derives from the right to withhold their collective labor—in short, the socialist systems do not tolerate an effective right to strike. Workers in the socialist systems do strike, of course, but the strikes are short-lived and soon suppressed. The strike under socialism is mostly illegal and, just as important, illegitimate. It is not a routine sanction as it is in the West; it is perceived as a challenge to the established order (as, once in a great while, strikes in the West can become).

The ideological rationale of the socialist leadership is that there can be no legitimate adversarial interest asserted by workers in a workers' state. To be sure, socialism under a regime of scarcity cannot get along without cost discipline in the labor input. But a socialist, "comradely labor discipline" is a different sort of cost discipline. Bukharin and Preobrazhensky asserted in the then authoritative *ABC of Communism*. It is "not imposed and sustained by the masters, not imposed and sustained by the capitalist whip, but by the labor organizations themselves, by the factory committees, and the trade unions. . . . They are engaged upon their own affairs; the edifice they are constructing belongs to the workers" (Bukharin and Preobrazhensky [1922] 1969, 338–39). The other element of ideology is the supremacy of the Communist Party, which will not share power in applying the "objective laws" of social and economic development.

Understandably, the ideologies of the Soviet-type societies also do not allow for a management interest differentiated from the worker's interest, just as particular group interests cannot be permitted to diverge from the social interest as determined by the

Party. Accordingly, institutions through which such interests can be asserted or resolved—which is what Western industrial relations is mostly about—also bear the stigma of illegitimacy. The fact that the industrial cost discipline presents itself as a socialist discipline seems to make no difference to the workers who experience it, however. In consequence they feel more exploited than any Western working class because they have no legitimate channel through which to press their protest.

The work society in the socialist enterprise has fundamentally the same protective outlook as do work societies everywhere. What is different are the institutional means and their legitimacy through which the work societies may press their protectivism. Since organized and institutionalized sanctions are illegal and dangerous, the workers resort to a kind of sabotage, or what Veblen once called—referring to the IWW—the conscientious withdrawal of efficiency. As summarized by one authority on Soviet industrial relations, these underground sanctions include: "late arrivals at work, prolonged breaks, indifferent performance, moonlighting and drinking during working hours, work to rule, evasion and violation of formal norms, early quitting time, malingering, absenteeism from work, thefts of tools and materials in enterprises, passivity and non-attendance at meetings and production conferences, and high labour turnover' (Porket 1978, 79). To this list should be added wildcat strikes.

The Soviet-type trade unions, although conceptualized as autonomous institutions, are actually administrative instrumentalities of state power. Not unlike Western unions, they represent workers in certain types of grievances, including dismissals and poor working conditions. They also administer plant social services. The unions are encouraged to denounce managerial "bureaucratism" at the plant level (Ruble 1979, 236). But the resemblance ends there. Otherwise, the unions function as "levers and transmission belts" for the promotion of more efficient production. In order to weaken cohesion employees, staff, and managers are lumped together in the same plant level organization, which is directed from the very top down.

From the Party's viewpoint unions must be restrained from the pursuit of particularistic interests at the expense of the centrally planned goals. Just as important, unions have to be prevented from building power bases competitive with the Party's totalist control system.

> In the opinion of many, the trade unions fail to defend and assert the interests of their members and confine their activities to ensuring the implementation of tasks assigned from above; they display excessive submissiveness to the enterprise management, the state and the party and lack internal democracy. Further, it is widely felt that membership meetings of the trade union organizations, productivity conferences, and Socialist emulations are mostly useless and ineffective because of their empty formalism. (Porket 1978, 79)

There are some interesting and important deviations from type in the socialist systems. The most important is the Yugoslav system of self-management. This is not the place to synthesize the vast literature on the subject, a good deal of it written by the Yugoslavs themselves. This much can be said: Yugoslav self-management represents an unprecedented experiment in the decentralization of economic management in a centrally planned socialist system, just as self-management represents an unprecedented effort to enhance worker power in the socialist enterprise. But it is not *self*-management in a literal sense. Workers are sufficiently checked and balanced by staff, management, and the Party to make them, at best, junior partners in enterprise management.

Hungarian industrial relations deviate from the Soviet type in conceding the propriety of "differing individual group and local interests" and of conflicts arising therefrom. The practical effect has been to enlarge the autonomy and influence of unions somewhat, but "timidity and reluctance in fulfilling their interest-protecting role continue" (Porket 1975, 379).

Pluralism or more or less autonomous bargaining is viewed as so costly to economic goals in the socialist model that the state moves in to displace the parochial interests of the parties by a more "general," "public," or "socialist" interest. The democratic capitalisms allow the sectional interests to have enough legitimate power to bargain with the state and arrive at a consensus. Sectional interests by a working class are accorded neither legitimacy nor structured bargaining power in the socialist, nonmarket systems. This inevitably forces protest underground until a revolutionary challenge to the state erupts, which is then suppressed and the marshaling of forces for another confrontation begins all over again.

All work societies contain a large hard core of "natural" protectivism. If not given legitimate channels to travel through, protectivism goes underground or has to be controlled or suppressed by state power. Even if suppressed, protectivism is still capable of inflicting serious damage on productive efficiency simply because some workers' consent is indispensable in evoking an efficient productive effort.

The highly structured, bilateral, collective bargaining industrial relations systems seem to be associated with the highly developed industrialisms of North America and Western Europe. The statist-centered systems seem to be associated with the less-developed industrialisms. Given their respective goals, the advanced industrialisms have broader tolerances within which to operate than do the less developed, and so have more room for the exercise of discretion by participants in the work process. The advanced industrialisms also have ideologies, laws, and values which put a premium on discretion and participation.

# CHAPTER TEN

# Industrial Relations and Conflict

CONFLICT, LATENT OR MANIFEST, is the essence of industrial relations, but the object of industrial relations as technique is the *resolution* of the conflict. Conflict is the essence of industrial relations
because industrialism necessarily generates stratifications, which,
in turn, necessarily generate tensions among those stratified.

Tensions are innate to the industrial order, regardless of
whether it is a socialist or capitalist order. Tensions, we know,
spring from technology, scale, organization, efficiency, and uncertainty—the essential features of industrialism. These features necessarily generate tensions of command and subordination, competitiveness, exploitation, physical deprivation at work, and
economic insecurity. Industrial relations as technique consists
largely of resolving tensions in the interest of preserving a going
enterprise and humane working conditions.

Tensions are latent conflict which becomes overt in diverse
manifestations. The strike is only one manifestation, albeit the
most costly and the most visible.

The conflict "universe" consists of a variety of adversary interactions. The adversaries are, as we have seen, either unions versus
employers or employees versus employees and management versus
management. More recently the state has become a bargaining adversary seeking to influence the outcome of the labor transaction
between unions and employers.

The locus of conflict in which the adversaries operate is either
the bargaining table for the negotiation of the agreement or the
shop floor for the further negotiation or application of the agreement. The third locus of conflict is politics, where unions and employers pursue their adversary interests—and occasionally their

common interests—in the forum provided by the public policy debate.

Each locus of conflict has its characteristic instrumentality through which conflict is expressed. Collective bargaining typically produces the strike. The grievance and wildcat strikes spring from the union-management relationship on the shop floor; and absenteeism, quits, and indiscipline are manifestations of conflict in the informal work society. Political conflict generates election contests and legislative votes.

Conflict in industrial relations, or more often the threat of it, far from being pathological or aberrant, is normal and even necessary. The principle is that the parties can be kept "honest" only by countervailing checks and balances. Conflict looking toward resolution is like a stabilizer or governor which signals the parties away from extreme positions by confronting them with the likely costs.

Latent and manifest conflicts contain within them—to put it into the dialectical style—the seeds of their own resolution. Indeed, industrial conflict cannot be understood at all without a frame of reference that also includes conflict *resolution*. This is because in the bargaining context conflict is not an end itself but a means to an end: specifically, a means to induce agreement.

Bargaining is, as has been said by many, a cooperative form of conflict in which the parties—or for that matter the social partners—seek to exchange what they want from each other. Unlike competitors who seek to oust one another, bargainers seek a mutually agreeable exchange. Unions and managements compete only for the intangible value of employee loyalty. In fact, the parties to the labor transaction are tied to each other more than buyers and sellers of nonlabor commodities because alternate sources of labor supply and demand are much more difficult to come by.

In the perceptions of the parties collective bargaining is mostly an adversary game constrained at the margin only by their common interest in the size of the fund available for distribution to wages and profits. Yet the fundamental commonality which underlies the collective bargaining relationship is underscored by the preoccupation of the parties with the avoidance and rationalization of overt conflict.

Rationalization of conflict means that the parties have subsituted procedural and substantive rules for trial-by-ordeal and confrontation. The strike has gradually been divested of its confrontational aspect and, for many purposes, has been reduced to a sequence of symbolic gestures. Nonetheless, confrontation is never far from the surface. Rationalization does not imply that the differences which divide the parties are any less but that the differences are no longer asserted through physical encounters.

The concept of a generalized, overriding class struggle culminating in the triumph of the working class cannot find support in the evidence of collective bargaining. The first problem with the concept has to do with the dispersion of adversarial relationships, which are as likely to encompass employees versus employees or the states versus unions and employers as they are the classic unions versus employers. The second problem has to do with the pressures on unions and employers to conciliate their conflicts, making it difficult to sustain a posture of permanent warfare. The final problem is that both unions and employers have been able to advance their respective interests under the regime of bargaining, thereby avoiding the catastrophes of immiseration and diminishing profits which Marx had designed to bring about capitalism's downfall. Indeed, a sort of neo-Marxism has emerged which denigrates the revolutionary potential of advanced capitalism's working class precisely because bargaining has *not* led to revolution.

The intellectual problem is how to deal with conflict as an analytical category. Essentially the problem comes to this: how can "normal" conflict be distinguished from "pathological" conflict? Normal conflict is the conflict essential to the maintenance of the system and without which the system is largely incapable of functioning. Pathological (or dysfunctional) conflict is not only *not* essential to the maintenance of the system, it may even be destructive of it.

Although conflict is an element in the maintenance of equilibrium in the industrial relations system, there is a point beyond which conflict becomes "aberrant," "abnormal," "dysfunctional," or "pathological," or whatever the right word is. It is not yet possible to determine analytically the nature of the boundary, the point at which conflict is normal or abnormal at an abstract level of theory.

But a rudimentary beginning may be made in the direction of a general theory by examining particular cases. The method here has been to make a quick mental inventory of what have been, by common consent, some of the "horrible examples" of industrial conflict in recent times and to work up stepwise to a more general formulation of aberrant conflict.

The following are examples of "deviant" conflict behavior:

1. Conflict accompanied by pervasive violence.
2. Conflict which results in wholesale disorganization of community or society.
3. Conflict which is associated with extinction of unions or managements as institutions.
4. The persistence of unhealthy and unsafe work environments.
5. The persistence of a large hard-core of absenteeism, tardiness, and indiscipline through periods of economic expansion and contraction.
6. Long-term declining productivity not caused by corresponding improvement in work quality.
7. The inability of workers to maintain internal unity because of fragmentation, as indicated by persistent wildcat strikes and acute internal rivalries.
8. The permanent cooptation or manipulation of one side by the other.
9. The exclusion of important segments of the work force from representation and participation in the union or the work society.
10. The blocking of access to fair and efficient representation by bureaucracy, including excessive professionalism.
11. Persistent civil disobedience in an essentially democratic political system.

In more general terms, conflict pathology is conflict in contexts of violence, class warfare, social disorganization, alienating and life-threatening work environments, low productivity, cooptation, manipulation and fragmentation, and gross inequalities in income and power, all of which have to be present in some egregious way to qualify as pathology. The essential common ground occupied by all of these manifestations of conflict pathology are (1) the substantial impairment of the parties' representational capabilities, (2) major impairment of the public interest in the process of asserting sectional claims, and (3) infringement of basic human rights to be free from violence to the person and life-threatening stress at work.

In sum, the logic of our argument runs as follows:

1. The wage relationship under collective bargaining is a species of exchange in which human effort is exchanged for a wage.
2. The labor transaction under collective bargaining involves both congruence and incongruence—congruence because one side wants something from the other, incongruence because the sides invariably differ on the relative values which should prevail.
3. In order to generalize validly as to whether the exchange relationship in the case of the labor transaction is generating *undue* conflict the following intermediate theories are required:
   a. A theory of the universe of conflict which takes into account not only strikes but turnover, absenteeism, sabotage, indiscipline or latent tendencies with these results.
   b. A theory of latent and overt conflict.
   c. A theory of conflict pathology; that is, when does conflict become dysfunctional?

This groping toward a theory of conflict and its pathology is not intended to suggest blame and merit for one side or another. Only rarely are there heroes and villians in industrial relations. Nor are we necessarily making a judgment as to whether normality or pathology represent inferior or superior, lower or higher stages. They may very well be one or the other, but this depends on how the "higher" purpose is defined. If the object is a going industrial relations system, however, then tension and conflict must be assumed as given, and the essential industrial relations technique, or art, consists in understanding and managing that tension and conflict. Pathological conflict can destroy or endanger the system.

This line of argument is meant to address two realities of industrial relations: (1) the tendency of bargaining antagonists committed to the existing industrial relations order to, nevertheless, press their conflict to the point of dysfunction; (2) the tendency to impute dysfunction to conflict which is, in fact, functional. The latter is a misconception of both the right and the left. On the right the tendency is to mistake the absence of overt conflict as an indicator of management effectiveness or to overlook the significance of certain forms of shop-floor behavior (quits, for example) as conflict. On the left the tendency is to see any escalation of industrial conflict as the herald of the "final conflict."

Beyond conflict is the utopian vision of workplace relationships governed by altruism and trust—that is, by nonexchange considerations. One suspects that some measure of power parity is a first condition for this version of utopia. The negative imprint which Marx and Engels have put on the utopian mode of speculation ought not to deter additional reflection.

J. Douglas Brown put it this way a generation ago: Industrial relations "is the study of values arising in the minds, intuitions and emotions of individuals" (Brown 1952, 6). To follow through: In a liberal society the business of industrial relations is technique and know-how, but it is more than that. It is also the values toward which technique and know-how strive. Equity, due process, fairness, just cause, rights, problem solving, reasonableness, participation, incentive, "disalienation," privacy, democracy, self-determination, good faith, mutual survival, incrementalism, pragmatism, job satisfaction, order, social responsibility—these are some of the values which are imbedded into the daily practice of industrial relations.

These values are more important than any putative industrial relations "science." They are more important than capitalism and socialism. No industrial relations problem of any importance turns on capitalism versus socialism, as we are learning at the moment from the drama which the Polish workers are unfolding before our eyes. Motivation, alienation, low productivity, poor supervision, the deteriorating work ethic, absenteeism—all of what we think of as dysfunctions of industrial relations, and indeed, the adversary principle as such—are problems of *all* modern industrial societies.

This must be because the dysfunctions are a consequence of the industrializing process as such and not alone of the juridical system under which it operates.

To finish up: Industrial relations as a field of study, like most of the social sciences, needs to liberate itself from obsessive reliance on mechanistic counting and theorizing, and return to the values of the founding fathers of industrial relations, who, if I am not mistaken, tried to get at the *spirit* of industrial relations. I close with a text in point from John R. Commons, who must rank as *the* founding father: "There can be no question of reasonableness in maximum net income economics. It is only a question of economic power. But the institutional economics of willingness takes into account the ethical use of economic power" (Commons 1936, 240).

BIBLIOGRAPHY
INDEX

# Bibliography

American Management Association [AMA]. 1974. *Flexible Work Time: Can It Work for You?* Announcement of Conference. New York, September 17, 1974.

———.1980. "The Non-Union Employer: Preventive Labor Relations." Course Prospectus. New York.

Baldamus, W. 1961. *Efficiency and Effort.* London: Social Science Paperbacks, in association with Tavistock Publications.

Barbash, Jack. 1956. *Practice of Unionism.* New York: Harper.

Barnett, George E. 1933. "Presidential Address." *American Economic Review,* March.

Blauner, Robert. 1960. "Work Satisfaction and Trends in Modern Industrial Society." In *Labor and Trade Unionism,* ed. Walter Galenson and Seymour Martin Lipset. New York: Wiley.

Blumberg, Paul. 1969. *Industrial Democracy: The Sociology of Participation.* New York: Schocken.

Bognanno, Mario F., and Kim, Sookon. 1981. "Collective Bargaining in Korea." *Proceedings of the Industrial Relations Research Association* [IRRA].

Bok, Derek C., and Dunlop, John T. 1970. *Labor and the American Community.* New York: Simon and Schuster.

Boulding, Kenneth. 1953. *The Organizational Revolution.* New York: Harper.

Brown, J. Douglas. 1952. "University Research in Industrial Relations." *Proceedings of the IRRA.*

Bücher, Carl. 1919. "The Factory System." In *Current Economic Problems,* ed. Walton H. Hamilton. Chicago: Univ. of Chicago Press.

Bukharin, N., and Preobrazhensky, E. [1922] 1969. *The ABC of Communism.* Baltimore: Penguin.

*Business Week.* 1966. "Putting a Dollar Sign on Everything," July 16.

———. 1977. "What Undid Jarman: Paperwork Paralysis," January 24.

Chamberlain, Neil. 1960. "Issues for the Future." *Proceedings of the IRRA.*

———. 1962. *The Firm: Micro-Economic Planning in Action.* New York: McGraw-Hill.

———. 1965. *The Labor Sector.* New York: McGraw-Hill.

———. 1967. "Strikes in a Contemporary Context." *Industrial and Labor Relations Review,* July.

————. 1968. "Unions and the Managerial Process." In *Technology, Industry, and Man,* ed. C. R. Walker. New York: McGraw-Hill.

Chamberlain, Neil, and Kuhn, James W. 1965. *Collective Bargaining.* 2nd ed. New York: McGraw-Hill.

Clark, Kenneth. 1969. "The Negro and the Urban Crisis." In *Agenda for the Nation,* ed. Kermit Gordon. Washington: Brookings Inst.

Cobbs, John. 1975. "When Companies Get Too Big to Fail." *Business Week,* January 27.

Collier, Ruth Berns, and Collier, David. 1979. "Inducement versus Constraints: Disaggregating 'Corporatism,' " *American Political Science Review* 73 (December).

Commons, John R. 1919. *Industrial Goodwill.* New York: McGraw-Hill.

————. 1921. "Industrial Relations." In *Trade Unionism and Labor Problems.* Boston: Ginn.

————. 1923. "American Shoemakers, 1648–1895." In *Labor and Administration.* New York: Macmillan.

————. 1924. *Legal Foundations of Capitalism.* New York: Macmillan.

————. 1936. "Institutional Economics." *American Economic Review,* Supplement, March.

Cox, Archibald. 1973. Quoted in D. E. Feller, "A General Theory of the Collective Bargaining Agreement. *California Law Review* 61 X (May).

Craft, James A. 1975. "Human Resource Accounting and Manpower Management." *Journal of Economics and Business* (Univ. of Illinois), Fall.

Crittenden, Ann. 1976. "Closing in on Corporate Payoffs Overseas." *New York Times,* February 15.

Crozier, Michael. 1969. "A New Rationale for American Business." *Perspectives on American Business, Daedalus,* Winter.

Dalton, Melville. 1959. *Men Who Manage.* New York: Wiley.

Davis, Louis E., and Taylor, James C., eds. 1972. *Design of Jobs.* London: Penguin.

Dennison, Edward F. 1962. *The Sources of Economic Growth and the Alternatives before Us.* New York: Committee for Economic Development.

————. 1979. "Explanations of Declining Productivity Growth." *Survey of Current Business,* August.

Drucker, Peter. 1962. *The New Society.* New York: Harper & Row.

————. 1964. *The Concept of the Corporation.* New York: New American Library.

Dunlop, John T. 1967. "The Function of the Strike." In *Frontiers of Collective Bargaining,* ed. John T. Dunlop and Neil W. Chamberlain. New York: Harper & Row.

————. 1973. "Predictions on Trends in Industrial Relations." *Labor Relations Reporter,* vol. 84.

————. 1976. "The Limits of Legal Compulsion." *Labor Law Journal,* February.

Eckstein, Otto. 1926. "Econometric Models and the Formation of Business Expectations." *Challenge*, March–April.

Essenberg, Bert. 1981. "The Interaction of Industrial Relations and the Political Process in Developing Countries: A Review of the Literature." *Labour and Society* 6 (January–March).

Etzioni, Amitai. 1964. *Modern Organizations.* Englewood Cliffs, N.J.: Prentice-Hall.

Fayol, Henri. [1908] 1970. Quoted in *Management Thinkers,* ed. A. Tillett, T. Kemone, and G. Wills. Baltimore: Penguin.

Feller, David E. 1973. "A General Theory of the Collective Bargaining Agreement." *California Law Review* 61 X (May).

Flanders, Allan. 1968. "Collective Bargaining: A Theoretical Analysis." *British Journal of Industrial Relations,* March.

Fleming, R. W. 1968. *The Labor Arbitration Process.* Urbana: Univ. of Illinois Press.

Ford, Henry, in collaboration with Crowther, Samuel. [1922]1965. *My Life and Work,* quoted in Alfred Chandler, Jr., *Giant Enterprise.* New York: MacFaddan.

Foulkes, Fred K. 1980. "Large Nonunionized Employers." In *U.S. Industrial Relations, 1950–80: A Critical Assessment,* ed. J. Stieber et al. Madison, Wis: IRRA.

Fox, Alan. 1971. *A Sociology of Work in Industry.* London: Collier-Macmillan.

Freedman, Audrey. 1982. "A Fundamental Change in Wage Bargaining." *Challenge,* August.

Freeman, Richard B. 1982. "Labor Studies." *Reporter* (National Bureau of Economic Research), Summer.

Fried, Marc A. 1966. "Role of Work in a Mobile Society." In *Planning for a Nation of Cities,* ed. S. B. Warner. Cambridge: MIT Press.

Fuller, Stephen H. 1980. "How Quality-of-Worklife Projects Work for General Motors." *Monthly Labor Review,* July.

Galbraith, John Kenneth. 1968. *The New Industrial State.* New York: New American Library.

Gardner, Burleigh. 1946. *Human Relations in Industry.* Chicago: Irwin.

General Motors Corporation. 1978. *Statement on the Changing Work Environment.* Report submitted to the Joint Economic Committee of the Congress of the United States. Washington, June 28.

Gladstone, Alan. 1979. "Trade Unions, Growth, and Development." International Industrial Relations Association, Geneva.

Goldberg, Arthur J. 1966. Quoted in H. S. Roberts, "Toward an Understanding of the Public Interest in Collective Bargaining." In *The Labor Movement: A Re-Examination,* ed. Jack Barbash. Madison, Wis.: IRRI.

Goldthorpe, John H., et al. 1968. *The Affluent Worker: Industrial Attitudes and Behavior.* Cambridge: Cambridge Univ. Press.

*Bibliography*

————. 1969. *The Affluent Worker in the Class Structure.* Cambridge: Cambridge Univ. Press.

Goodwin, Leonard. 1972. *Do the Poor Want to Work?* Washington: Brookings Inst.

Gregory, Charles O. 1961. *Labor and the Law.* New York: Norton.

Grether, E. T. 1966. *Marketing and Public Policy.* Englewood Cliffs, N.J.: Prentice-Hall.

Halberstam, David. 1973. *The Best and the Brightest.* Greenwich, Conn.: Fawcett-Crest.

Harbison, Fred, and Coleman, John. 1951. *Goals and Strategy in Collective Bargaining.* New York: Harper.

Hare, A.E.C. 1965. *The First Principles of Industrial Relations.* New York: St. Martin's.

Heller, Walter. 1967. *New Dimensions of Political Economy.* New York: Norton.

Herrick, Neal Q., and Quinn, Robert P. 1971. "The Working Conditions Survey as a Source of Social Indicators." *Monthly Labor Review,* April.

Herzberg, Frederick. 1970. "The Motivation-Hygiene Theory." In *Management and Motivation,* ed. Victor H. Vroom and Edward L. Deci. Baltimore: Penguin.

Hitch, Charles. 1967. "Program Planning and Budgeting." In *Planning, Programming, and Budgeting.* U.S. Senate, Subcommittee on National Security and International Operations, Committee on Government Operations.

Holton, Richard H. 1969. "Business and Government." *Perspectives on Business, Daedalus* (Cambridge, Mass.), Winter.

Homans, G. C. 1961. *Social Behavior: Its Elementary Forms.* New York: Harcourt, Brace.

Hooper, Frederic. 1960. *Management Survey.* London: Pelican.

Hoxie, Robert. 1923. *Trade Unionism in the United States.* New York: Appleton.

Ingram, J. K. [1894] 1965. Quoted in Sidney and Beatrice Webb, *The History of British Trade Unionism.* Reprint of 1894 ed. New York: Kelley.

Ishikawa, Akihiro. 1982. "A Survey of Seven Studies in the Japanese Style of Management." *Economic and Industrial Democracy* (Stockholm) 3 (February).

Janis, Irving L., and Mann, Leon. 1977. Quoted in Christopher Jencks, "Decisions, Decisions," a review of *Decision Making: A Psychological Analysis of Conflict, Choice, and Commitment* by Irving L. Janis and Leon Mann. *New York Times Book Review,* July 3.

Jautcher, Gerald R. 1973. *Federal Aids to the Maritime Industries.* Washington: Brookings Inst.

Jensen, M. C. 1975. "Corporate Corruption Is Big Business." *New York Times,* September 14.

Jerome, William T., III. 1970. "Kinds of Control." In *Readings in Management.* ed. Ernest Dale. New York: McGraw-Hill.

Johnson, Lyndon B. 1969. Quoted in *AFL-CIO News,* January 18.

Johri, C. K. 1967. *Unionism in a Developing Economy.* New Delhi: Asia Publishing.

Juris, Hervey A., and Roomkin, Myron, 1980. *The Shrinking Perimeter.* Lexington, Mass.: Lexington Books.

Kahn, Robert L. 1958. "Human Relations on the Shop Floor." In *Human Relations and Modern Management,* ed. E. M. Hugh-Jones. Amsterdam: North-Holland.

Karnik, V. B. 1969. *Indian Trade Unions: A Survey,* quoted in Everett M. Kassalow, *Trade Unions and Industrial Relations.* New York: Random House.

Kassalow, Everett M. 1969. *Trade Unions and Industrial Relations.* New York: Random House.

Katona, George. 1963. *Psychological Analysis of Economic Behavior.* New York: McGraw-Hill.

Kaufman, Bruce E. 1982. "Determinants of Strikes." *Industrial and Labor Relations Review* 35 (July).

Kennedy, John F. 1962. Quoted in *New York Times,* June 12.

Kerr, Clark, ed. 1964. *Labor and Management in Industrial Society.* New York: Doubleday-Anchor.

Khatkhate, Deena R. 1971. "Management in Developing Countries." *Finance and Development Quarterly,* 3.

Kirkland, Lane. 1976. Quoted in "Labor's Role in Politics Keyed to Inpendent Union Policies." *AFL-CIO News,* October 2.

Knight, Frank H. [1921] 1957. *Risk, Uncertainty, and Profit.* 8th impression. London: London School of Economics.

Koontz, Harold, and O'Donnell, Cyril, 1968. *Management: A Book of Readings.* New York: McGraw-Hill.

Kuhn, James W. 1961. *Bargaining in Grievance Settlement.* New York: Columbia Univ. Press.

――――. 1967. "The Grievance Process." In *Frontiers of Collective Bargaining,* ed. John T. Dunlop and Neil W. Chamberlain. New York: Harper & Row.

――――. 1980. "Electrical Products." In *Collective Bargaining: Contemporary American Experience,* ed. Gerald G. Somers. Madison, Wis.: IRRA.

Lawler, Edward E., III. 1970. "Job Design and Employee Motivation." In *Management and Motivation. See* Herzberg 1970.

Leiserson, William M. [1931] 1969. "The Economics of Restriction of Output. In *Restriction of Output among Unorganized Workers,* ed. S. B. Mathewson. Carbondale: Southern Illinois Univ. Press.

Lenin, V. I. [1902] 1943. *What Is To Be Done?* New York: International Pub.

Levitan, Sar A., and Johnson, William B. 1973. *Work Is Here to Stay, Alas.* Salt Lake City: Olympus.

Lewis, Flora. 1981. "The American Ailment," a summary of "Le Mal Americain" by Michael Crozier. *New York Times,* January 19.

Likert, Rensis. 1967. *The Human Organization: Its Management and Value.* New York: McGraw-Hill.

————. 1970. "New Patterns of Management." In *Management and Motivation. See* Herzberg 1970.

Malthus, Thomas R. [1798] 1956. Quoted in Reinhard Bendix, *Work and Authority in Industry.* New York: Wiley.

Marceau, LeRoy, ed. 1969. *Dealing with a Union.* New York: American Management Assoc.

Marshall, Alfred. [1890] 1948. *Principles of Economics.* 8th ed. New York: Macmillan.

Martin, Norman H., and Sims, John H. 1964. "Power Tactics." In *Readings in Managerial Psychology,* ed. Harold J. Leavitt and Louis R. Pondy. Chicago: Univ. of Chicago Press. Originally published in *Harvard Business Review,* November–December 1956.

Mathewson, S. B., ed. [1931] 1969. *Restriction of Output among Unorganized Workers.* Carbondale: Southern Illinois Univ. Press.

Maslow, A. H. [1943] 1970. "A Theory of Human Motivation." In *Management and Motivation. See* Herzberg 1970.

Mayo, Elton. [1919] 1970. "Social Growth and Social Disintegration." In *Readings in Management,* ed. Ernest Dale. New York: McGraw-Hill.

McCarthy, W. E. J. 1969. "Collective Bargaining in Perspective." Trade Union Seminar on New Perspectives in Collective Bargaining. Paris: Organization for Economic Cooperation and Development. Mimeographed.

McDonald, John. 1970. "How Social Responsibility Fits the Game of Business." *Fortune,* December.

McMurry, R. N. 1967. "War and Peace in Labor Relations." In *Unions, Management, and the Public,* ed. E. Wight Bakke, Clark Kerr, and Charles Anrod. New York: Harcourt, Brace and World.

Mehta, Asoka. 1957. "The Mediating Role of the Trade Union in Underdeveloped Countries." In *Economic Development and Cultural Change.* Chicago: Univ. of Chicago Press.

Meyerson, Adam. 1982. "The Best and the Brightest Eye the Economy," a review of *Minding America's Business* by Ira C. Magaziner and Robert B. Reich. *Wall Street Journal,* March 31.

Miles, Raymond E. 1974. "Organization Development." In *Organizational Behavior, Research, and Issues,* ed. George Strauss et al. Madison, Wis.: IRRA.

Mills, D. Quinn. 1980. "Construction." In *Collective Bargaining: Contemporary American Experience,* ed. Gerald G. Somers. Madison, Wis.: IRRA.

Morse, Nancy C., and Weiss, Robert S. 1970. "The Function and Meaning of Work and the Job." In *Management and Motivation. See* Herzberg 1970.

National Industrial Conference Board [NICB]. 1963. "Employee Motivation—What Role for Personnel," *Management Record,* September.

Opsahl, Robert L., and Dunnette, Marvin D. 1970. "The Role of Financial Compensation in Industrial Motivation." In *Management and Motivation. See* Herzberg 1970.

Ozanne, Robert. 1967. *A Century of Labor-Management Relations at McCormick and International Harvester.* Madison: Univ. of Wisconsin Press.

Paladino, Morris. 1979. "Unions in Asia: Ten Years of Concern." AFL-CIO *American Federationist,* July.

Parisi, Anthony J. 1978. "Management: GE's Search for Synergy." *New York Times,* April 16.

Perlman, Selig. [1928] 1949. *A Theory of the Labor Movement.* Reprint of 1928 ed. New York: Augustus Kelley.

Pestillo, Peter J. 1979. "Learning to Live without a Union." *Proceedings of the IRRA.*

Porket, J. L. 1975. "Participation in Management in Communist Systems in the 1970's." *British Journal of Industrial Relations,* November.

———. 1978. "Industrial Relations and Participation in Management in the Soviet-Type Communist Systems." *British Journal of Industrial Relations,* March.

Prasow, Paul, and Peters, Edward. 1970. *Arbitration and Collective Bargaining.* New York: McGraw-Hill.

Price, Don K. 1968. "Science, the New Technologies, and Government," quoted in Charles R. Walker. *Technology, Industry, and Man.* New York: McGraw-Hill.

Rehn, Gösta. 1957. "Unionism and Wage Structure in Sweden." In *The Theory of Wage Determination,* ed. John Dunlop. New York: St. Martin's.

Rivlin, Alice M. 1971. *Systematic Thinking for Social Action.* Washington: Brookings Inst.

Rogers, Daniel. 1978. *Work Ethic in Industrial America, 1850–1920.* Chicago: Univ. of Chicago Press.

Ross, Arthur M. 1948. *Trade Union Wage Policy.* Berkeley: Univ. of California Press.

Ross, Ian, and Zander, Alvin. 1970. "Need Satisfactions and Employee Turnover." In *Management and Motivation. See* Herzberg 1970.

Rostow, W. W. 1960. *The Stages of Economic Growth.* Cambridge: Cambridge Univ. Press.

Ruble, Blair A. 1979. "Dual Functioning Trade Unions in the USSR." *British Journal of Industrial Relations* (July).

Runciman, Walter. 1966. *Relative Deprivation and Social Justice.* Berkeley: Univ. of California Press.

Samoff, Bernard. 1970. "Law School Education in NLRB Representation Cases." *Labor Law Journal,* November.

Sayles, Leonard R. 1958. *Behavior of Industrial Work Groups.* New York: Wiley.

Schelling, Thomas C. 1963. *The Strategy of Conflict.* New York: Oxford Univ. Press.

Schumacher, E. F. 1973. *Small Is Beautiful.* New York: Harper Torchbooks.

Schumpeter, Joseph A. 1947. *Capitalism, Socialism, and Democracy.* New York: Harper.

Selekman, Benjamin M. 1947. *Labor Relations and Human Relations.* New York: McGraw-Hill.

Selznick, Philip. 1969. *Law, Society, and Industrial Justice.* New York: Russell Sage.

Serrin, William. 1969. "At Ford Everyone Knows Who Is the Boss." *New York Times Magazine,* October 19.

Sheppard, Harold, and Herrick, Neil. 1973. *Where Have All the Robots Gone?* New York: Free Press.

Shimada, Haru. 1980. *The Japanese Employment System.* Tokyo: Institute of Labor.

Shonfeld, Andrew. 1969. "Business in the Twenty-First Century." *Perspectives on Business, Daedalus,* Winter.

Schultz, George P. 1968. "Priorities in Policy and Research for Industrial Relations." *Proceedings of the IRRA.*

Siegel, Irving H., and Weinberg, Edgar. 1982. *Labor-Management Cooperation.* Kalamazoo: Upjohn.

Silk, Leonard. 1972. "Why Overruns in the Defense Market?" *New York Times,* April 19.

Simon, Herbert. 1959. "Theories of Decisionmaking in Economics and Behavioral Science." *American Economic Review,* June.

Sloan, Alfred P., Jr. 1965. *My Years with General Motors.* New York: Macfadden.

Smith, William H. 1959. *Current Trends in Collective Bargaining.* Berkeley: Institute of Industrial Relations, Univ. of California.

Spero, Sterling, and Capozzolla, John M. 1972. *The Urban Community and Its Unionized Bureaucracies.* New York: Dunnellen.

Strauss, George. 1964. "Organization Man: Prospect for the Future." *California Management Review,* Spring.

———. 1972. "Management by Objective: A Critical View." *Trade and Development Journal,* April.

Strauss, George, and Sayles, Leonard R. 1960. *Personnel.* Englewood Cliffs, N.J.: Prentice-Hall.

Tannenbaum, Arnold S. 1966. *Social Psychology of the Work Organization.* Belmont, Calif.: Wadsworth.

Tannenbaum, Frank. 1951. *A Philosophy of Labor.* New York: Knopf.

Taylor, Frederick W. [1911] 1947. *Scientific Management.* New York: Harper.

Taylor, Stuart, Jr. 1981. "Execution of a Union." *New York Times,* September 19.

Trades Union Congress [TUC]. 1966. *Trade Unionism.* London: TUC.

Trist, Eric. 1976. "Critique of Scientific Management in Terms of Socio-Technical Theory." In *Job Satisfaction,* ed. M. Weir. London: Fontana.

————. 1981. *The Evolution of Socio-Technical Systems.* Occasional Paper no. 2. Ontario: Ontario Ministry of Labor, June.

*United Steelworkers [USW] v. Warrior Gulf and Navigation Co.,* 363 U.S. 574, 579-80 (1960).

U.S. Bureau of Labor Statistics [USBLS]. 1964.

————. 1965. *Glossary of Current Industrial Relations and Wage Terms.* Bulletin 1438.

————. 1980. *Directory of National Unions and Employee Associations, 1979.* Washington: USDL.

U.S. Cabinet Committee on Price Stability. 1969. *Studies by the Staff of the Cabinet Committee on Price Stability.* Washington: GPO, January.

U.S. Department of Labor [USDL]. 1970. *Manpower Report of the President.* Washington: GPO, March.

U.S. National Mediation Board. 1950. *Fifteen Years under the Railway Labor Act, 1934-1949.* Washington: GPO.

Walker, Charles R. 1968. *Technology, Industry, and Man.* New York: McGraw-Hill.

Walker, Charles R., and Guest, Robert H. 1952. *The Man on the Assembly Line.* Cambridge: Harvard Univ. Press.

Walton, Richard E., and McKersie, Robert B. 1965. *A Behavioral Theory of Labor Negotiations.* New York: McGraw-Hill.

Ware, Norman J. [1924] 1964. *The Industrial Worker, 1840-1860.* Chicago: Quadrangle.

Weber, Max. [1920] 1958. *The Protestant Ethic and the Spirit of American Capitalism.* New York: Scribners.

Weidenbaum, Murray. 1981. Quoted in Leonard Silk, "Reagan Goals and Labor." *New York Times,* September 18.

Wellington, Harry H. 1968. *Labor and the Legal Process.* New Haven: Yale Univ. Press.

Westphal, Larry E. 1982. "The Private Sector as 'Principal Engine' of Development: Korea." *Finance and Development* (June).

Whiting, Basil. 1972. *Worker Alienation.* Testimony in hearings before the U.S. Senate Subcommittee on Employment, Manpower and Poverty, 92nd Cong., 2nd sess.

Whyte, William F. 1955. *Money and Motivation.* New York: Harper.

————. 1969. *Organizational Behavior.* Homewood, Ill.: Irwin-Dorsey.

Wiener, Norbert. 1954. *The Human Use of Human Beings.* 2nd ed. rev. New York: Doubleday-Anchor.

Wilensky, Harold. 1966. In *Labor in a Changing America,* ed. William Haber. New York: Basic Books.

Witte, Edwin E. 1932. *The Government in Labor Disputes.* New York: McGraw-Hill.

Woll, Mathew. 1960. Quoted in Robert D. Papkin, "Craft Unit vs. Industrial Unit Bargaining under the National Labor Relations Act." *George Washington Law Review,* December.

Woodward, Joan. 1966. *Management and Technology.* London: HMSO.

Young, Arthur. [1835] 1965. *Travels in France,* quoted in Phyllis Deane, *The First Industrial Revolution.* Cambridge: Cambridge Univ. Press.

# Index

TEXT DESIGNED BY ED FRANK
COMPOSED BY THE COMPOSING ROOM
KIMBERLY, WISCONSIN
MANUFACTURED BY CUSHING-MALLOY, INC.
ANN ARBOR, MICHIGAN

Library of Congress Cataloging in Publication Data
Barbash, Jack.
The elements of industrial relations.
Bibliography: pp. 139–148.
Includes Index.
1. Industrial relations. I. Title.
HD6971.B34     1984       331       83-40258
ISBN 0-299-09610-6
ISBN 0-299-09614-9 (pbk.)